T0067405

Freespirit

Freespirit

At Last
I Am Free
to Be
Me

WITH LOVE AND LIGHT

REVEREND JUDITH
WILKINSON-ZORNIG, MMSc

INTRODUCING: The Lady of The Golden Rose

BALBOA.
PRESS

A DIVISION OF HAY HOUSE

Copyright © 2013 Reverend Judith Wilkinson-Zornig, MMSc

All rights reserved. No part of this book may be used or reproduced by any means, graphic, electronic, or mechanical, including photocopying, recording, taping or by any information storage retrieval system without the written permission of the publisher except in the case of brief quotations embodied in critical articles and reviews.

Balboa Press books may be ordered through booksellers or by contacting:

Balboa Press
A Division of Hay House
1663 Liberty Drive
Bloomington, IN 47403
www.balboapress.com.au
1-(877) 407-4847

ISBN: 978-1-4525-0971-6 (sc)
ISBN: 978-1-4525-0972-3 (e)

Because of the dynamic nature of the Internet, any web addresses or links contained in this book may have changed since publication and may no longer be valid. The views expressed in this work are solely those of the author and do not necessarily reflect the views of the publisher, and the publisher hereby disclaims any responsibility for them.

The author of this book does not dispense medical advice or prescribe the use of any technique as a form of treatment for physical, emotional, or medical problems without the advice of a physician, either directly or indirectly. The intent of the author is only to offer information of a general nature to help you in your quest for emotional and spiritual well-being. In the event you use any of the information in this book for yourself, which is your constitutional right, the author and the publisher assume no responsibility for your actions.

Any people depicted in stock imagery provided by Thinkstock are models, and such images are being used for illustrative purposes only.
Certain stock imagery © Thinkstock.

Printed in the United States of America

Balboa Press rev. date: 04/01/2013

Dedication

To my best friend Neville Hope,

Thank you for your support and assistance with this book.

You are the one person who understands me and

have been my source

of inspiration and motivation.

You continue to give me insight in my life's purpose.

And to . . . The Lady of the Golden Rose

Table of Contents

Foreword
Life is a Journey, of Growth and Expansion

Sometimes a book is written that forever changes not only the way we think about life, but also the way we feel about life. This is *FREESPIRIT At last I am free to be Me.* Not only does it open our minds, it opens our hearts. The book is about life as a journey as 't is expressed through love for the self.

May you be challenged and blessed with this book as I have.

Thank you Judy.

"Who am I?" and, "What's it all about?"

There comes at least one time in life when one asks these questions.

To find the answers to these and many more questions has been my focus all of this life and at long last, I believe I have a handle on them. I can't say, that this is it, everyone take note. But I can say for this part of my life, that these insights are working for myself and many people I read for and help in my busy life as a Psychic Clairvoyant and Channel. I wouldn't be the first or the last person to say I have had a challenging life. And I certainly am not the only person to say that I have created situations, that I didn't believe could be resolved or even that I thought I could survive and live to see another bright and happy day. Well here I am. I have experienced life's best and what seemed like life's worst, but I know I will find people who have experienced far greater hardships, and also far greater successes and joys then what I myself have experienced. What I can say is that what I have experienced has never been boring and fortunately for me and my friends and associates, I have always at last been able to see the humorous side to every situation. Even when it has meant that I am the fool, the victim, the clown or just me.

The one thing I do want to impress on the readers of this book is that life is a journey, of growth and expansion. And the only way to get through it is to live it and enjoy it and allow it to unfold into the magic and wonderment and love that was always intended by our creator. Nothing leaves me in awe, as much as the synchronicity of events unfolding and the right people who appear in and out of life and situations at precisely the right timing. In synchronicity, sometimes life can actually feel like a very well scripted and award winning play, with outstanding directors to plan out the dramas and wonderful moments. Life is an adventure, experience it, live it and love it and then you will find the magic of love and who you are and what it is all about. ENJOY!

Foreward by Carmela Serratore.

Preface

The book is a compilation of Spiritual Insights that, to this day help even myself, when life gets a bit stuck or I become confused. This book takes you through the complete Healing Process from a complete breakdown and gives insight into becoming new and whole with the wisdom to understand and appreciate life and to understand God and Spirituality.

Throughout life, I think we all are perplexed at the choices that people make, people that we care about and interact with in our personal and professional lives, and sometimes we may feel let down, or disappointed, or betrayed, even to the point that we think that somebody, somewhere is out to get us, or that we were cursed, and who is God, and was there ever a God anyway, and why does he or it let people suffer so much? On the other hand, we can experience days that we think Heaven has devoured us and everything goes so wonderful and life can be an adventure full of wonderment and romance and joy, which can easily and suddenly be engulfed in devastation by people betraying us or someone close to us, or illness or even death.

This book gives insights into all kinds of situations, so that if a reader looks up a chapter there just maybe the few words of encouragement which will help them to lift out of a pit of despair and self pity, or confusion, that so many of us find ourselves in, while reinforcing in a very positive way, that we are guided, we are not alone and that there is a reason for everything that happens.

In this book, certain words have been capitalised to emphasise that they connate a source of power and highlight the significance of God and Spirituality.

*A*fter chasing rainbows for all of this life and possibly many other lifetimes, I have finally found the pot of gold. It was in my own heart all the time, and no, the grass is not greener anywhere else. As Dorothy in the Wizard of Oz once said, *"Everything I could ever wish for is in my own back yard"*. These are the insights I have grown to understand along my path to finding myself. I pray that these insights may help to encourage someone else along their spiritual path to Enlightenment and Ascension, without having to grow through the pain of bitter life lessons. However, I can now look back and see that the whole life's journey was worth every ounce of sweat, and every tear, for it is through enduring what life has to offer, that we do eventually come to the understanding and peace of knowing that everything was always, just the way it was meant to be, that God, our Guides, our Angels, never for a moment left us, that we are really the writer of our own script in life, and that these loving beings that surround us ethereally and in the real world, or should I say the Third or Fourth and Fifth Dimension, look after us, guide us, love us and protect us, constantly, for eternity and show great patience and love as we walk our path to find the love, and peace and joy in this world, in this lifetime. Life is truly a gift, enjoy your life, your adventure, for no matter where you are on your life journey, understand, that the loving beings and the "Light Beings" that orchestrated your life are constantly loving and guiding you . . . If you cannot see or feel them around you, go to a place in nature and sit and ponder, or meditate on how magnificent a miracle, a rose, a child, a breath of air really is, and then consider how magnificent you, yes, you and your life, and all the people in your life really are. And, when you have finished, ask yourself, *"Are you, your own best friend?"* *"Are you worthy of playing the leading role in your Life?"*

Introduction
Life is a Gift

As long ago as I can remember, probably when I was about four years old, I stood under a clear and beautiful, star filled night sky. Gazing as I often did, at the bright and twinkling lights in the heavens above. In those days, there wasn't any television to distract my inquisitive minds' ramblings, which allowed the freedom of an overactive imagination to roam the universe and all the realms without any barriers or blocks and few fears of monsters of the deep dark beyond. This conditioning comes into play later, being used as manipulation and control tactics, from people who should know better, but unfortunately, don't. Almost every night I would walk and sing and dance under the Heavens, with a very strange sense of wondering; *"Where am I? Who am I? And what on earth was I doing here?"* Well, I had one thing right, I was on Planet Earth. The bright lights of the stars glistened and seemingly were speaking to me, as if they knew all the answers. But the problem was, I had forgotten the code, I needed someone to translate the messages they were sending, I thought. And yet a deep inner most connection brought about a wondrous knowing, that those Heavens above, were where I belonged, and one of those stars was my real home, a whole other world and existence. How had I come to be standing here, watching galaxies and the universe dance before my very eyes when I belonged up there, dancing from one planet to another, singing and dancing my way through the Heavens upon Heavens. Freely exploring new horizons and new adventures and new experiences, always another adventure and another new reality never tired, never bored and certainly never weary.

Realizing now, beyond any dream, with my two feet firmly attached to Planet Earth, seemingly trapped in a body, so dense and lifeless. Oh stars and angels, please, please come and rescue me. Some days I would race around the back yard on the broom handle, which was really my racing stallion of long, long ago, racing wild and free with the nations of Navaho, Indian friends. The tribes from days gone by would come and join me and I would just for a moment, or a day, be free with the wind and spirit to keep me company.

Some days my kind brother, who didn't understand this strange melancholy child, who wished and fantasized about angels and fairies and people he could not see, would take me to a paddock near our house and we would fly kites together. High in the sky and my friend the wind would lift my kite so high, and I would hear the whispers from on high, "Remember, you can fly this high, oh to be this free, once again." How I wished that I were the kite soaring through the air with the greatest of ease, instead of the anchor, which held on tightly, so it couldn't escape my grip. *"Hold on tight, don't let it get away!"*

Luckily we lived in a small country town, and there were days when I could roam the fields early in the mornings and collect fresh mushrooms. This also reminded me of days long ago, when to Earth I did come as a fairy and elves and butterflies were once my true friends. There were many adventures, some were fun, but some were tragic. But I needed to experience it all, just as I have in this life, so that I can remember once and for all time; *"Who am I."*

My loving parents, could not understand why; I was so very different from my rivalling siblings, who clambered to them for love and support. But I wanted to be free and join the wind and the nature spirits and find my true home, wherever that could be. And so my journey began. Who was I and where did I come from and where did I belong, and why was I here? Imagination unsurpassed by anyone, I would hold tea parties with Duchesses and Dukes and dress up and play different roles, sometimes with other little friends, but mostly with me, and my invisible friends. I was never alone, and I would call on my friends from all different realms. The physical children I met seemed to fade out of my life when they discovered that I had other friends that they couldn't see, and really couldn't be a part of something that they could never understand. They treated me suspiciously, for I was different, but they couldn't understand how?

I lived in my own world, free from harsh words, lectures and realities and pleased when they would leave me be. But this world would always intrude in my magical world, until one day I was in so much trouble I asked my friends to never return—and they were gone until now. It was like an echo in my head, *"Who am I? Why am I here?"* It occurred to me that I must have sinned, I must have been bad and this was my punishment. I must have been truly bad for I was a prisoner it seemed, a child on Planet Earth; when my whole being cried out, *"I want to be free."*

This book is a collection of articles with life's insights, which I have put together as I have undergone my experiences of life's lessons. These insights are in many books I have read and have known and yet I have not understood, until I experienced them myself. I wished that somebody could explain life to me, but now I understand that this is the gift, to live life and to come to the understandings of one.

I do not claim to have written anything that has not been written before, but as you read these words and connect with the meanings, you will come to understand the beauty and the wisdom as you come to realize that we are all here, we are here seeking the same things, all wanting to know who we are and why we are here. With these understandings and realizations, I pray that you will connect with God, your guides, and your angels in Oneness, in peace and in Love.

I give thanks every day, for my wonderful friends, and teachers and co-actors on the stage of life, as they have played their part in this wonderful adventure, called Life and all the gifts and adventures that life has to offer. Life is a gift, enjoy it and most of all, Live it.

Every person is special and here to develop and share life's lessons. Be kind to those who may not have your understanding and be gracious when you are the one who does not understand. Let go of your preconceived ideas as to how life should be and allow everything to flow in its perfect timing. Love your life and those who share in its creation. May the love and light of spirit, the creator and whatever you believe in, shine down and bless your days on this planet and may you experience the magic that I have come to understand and love.

The final realization is short and simple, Life is a Gift, Live it—ENJOY IT.

Reverend Judith Wilkinson—Zornig

Love

I was musing, things are very sad and lonely

It just didn't seem worthwhile

A voice from my precious candle says

"Yes! It is so, you have come for love

Love makes it all worthwhile

The wind in the trees

The waves on the sand

The birds in the sky

They all search for Love

Love makes it all worthwhile

A smile from a stranger

A hug from a friend

The song in your heart

The fresh fragrance of the flowers

Love makes it ALL, worthwhile

The due drops on the grass

The raindrops on the roof

A warm winter's fireplace

The Rose in the Garden

The hand of a friend

Love makes it all worthwhile

Channelling

As a psychic, clairvoyant, and spiritual teacher, people often ask me what channelling is. Channelling is allowing spirit to merge with your mind and, in some instances, your body in order to bring information through to this realm from other realms of consciousness. A channel or medium simply relaxes and enters into an altered state of consciousness, which is attainable through practicing meditation. In this higher state of consciousness and awareness I may add, one can experience many different realms and spirit worlds. Realms and worlds of differing vibrations, colours, sounds and energies are available to the psychic traveller, this also includes what is known as astral travelling. Through meditation, one can still one's mind enough to allow communication to take place with deceased friends, relatives and also the spirit of a higher consciousness or evolution. Whilst in this state of peace and tranquillity, the medium may also experience the consciousness of higher intelligence of all the worlds in which spirit exists. It is not uncommon to contact a spirit guide or relative in these states of higher consciousness and to relay information that may help people in this world. As I said earlier, it is also quite easy to merge with another spirit, allowing that spirit to use the voice and body as a vehicle to communicate directly with other earth beings. The medium relaxes to an even greater level, which is like a trance state, and steps aside; so that another entity can enter and relay the messages it wishes. This is known as trans-channelling or being a trans-medium. Often the medium has no recollection of what has been said and has experienced a very peaceful, sometimes, picturesque and vivid time. Usually there are no ill effects to the body or the mind; however, if one has never experienced channelling before, this can allow cause for concern, and it is best practiced with the assistance of an experienced channel or medium.

Channelling can also take many other forms, such as spiritual healings; inspirational writings; psychic art and drawings; music- and song-writing or any inspired, usually creative activity. Spiritual healing is channelling energy or healing vibrations to another part of your body; or to another person or other people. Reiki is a form of spiritual healing; that uses symbols and the channelling of energy to other people and situations. Many forms of art, poetry, songs, and music are channelled. Sometimes, the medium is unaware as to where the information is coming from; he or she may just feel an urge to express themselves, writing beautiful verse or poetry and even books as well as songs with great depth and feeling. Usually, channelled works just flow and require very little thought or planning. More often than not, they have a special message that will reach and touch many people. Readings are usually channelled, particularly if the medium is contacting relatives who have passed over. These events are; actually seeing into the future or into past lives.

Some people have a natural affinity with the spirit world, or they have innate abilities to see into different realms, but even they may take on meditation and different courses to enhance and understand their abilities. When working with an experienced teacher, or medium, many more doorways can open up. This is even the case for the most gifted of mediums, psychics and channells. Through understanding different processes, healing one's own mind, emotions, and soul, many people explore different realms, and experiences with a goal of becoming healed. These experiences can lead to becoming a clear and perfect channel of the light. As people undergo different processes along what is quite often referred to as a spiritual path with the goal of enlightenment, or Christ consciousness; or even ascension, they experience many different facets of the human experience, and spiritual and psychic realms. These experiences help people to grow in their consciousness, awareness, and understanding.

I must add at this point that there are other energies and entities that may not be of the light; however, they too have their purpose in creation. One can find doorways into these realms as well, and quite often a light-worker will experience in some degree the negative or darker forces in order to accumulate greater experience and understanding. All of these experiences lead to greater knowledge and ultimately wisdom.

Remember that the journey that life takes you on and your experiences into the astral and spiritual worlds all come down to your intent and your perceptions of what is real. Always take personal responsibility for all of your experiences, whether they are pure entertainment or an opportunity to learn and grow. These experiences can shift perceptions, transform beliefs and negative conditioning causing blocks and fears, yielding results in the way you think and act. Understand that nothing can harm you unless you allow it, unless you give it power.

All people have an ability to communicate to the higher realms. This can be as simple as saying a prayer. All people have an ability to receive and channel information from these realms. Some may have naturally developed gifts:—others may have to learn meditation, yoga, or some form of relaxation to develop these skills. All can communicate with spirit if they can put their egos aside for a few moments and are open to existence in all of its many forms. The quickest method is through the heart. This is the most accurate and uninfluenced form of connection with other entities in any realm. The heart never lies, deceives, or tries to hurt anyone, including its owner. This is unlike the mind, which will even deceive itself if given half a chance. The mind delves into illusion very quickly and is unable to feel the consequences of its actions or thoughts. Meditation helps to slow the mind down; so that one may get just a glimpse of truth. Once the truth is penetrated, life can take on a whole new experience of grandeur. There is a reality, or truth, which does not change, alter, or grow. The truth is Truth and in order to attain that, which does not alter, we must rise above our personal perceptions. Our personal truth is our belief system. We need to enter into the light of the highest vibration or consciousness, into God's mind, to know and understand Truth, clear, precise Truth.

People suffer greatly after the loss of a loved one. Many may say it is the greatest pain they have experienced. This is learned through our society and conditioning:—it also stems from not understanding the process of life. Due to many different reasons, people are reluctant to get on with their lives when someone close has passed. Some of these reasons may include guilt, not living their own lives, or not taking responsibility for their own lives. Grief comes in many forms and for many reasons; and is experienced most of the time for selfish reasons. In Islamic traditions and some Eastern and ancient cultures, people celebrated the death of their loved ones passing on to the spirit world—or dreamtime,—as it is known in some cultures. They knew and understood that many of the hardships, tests, and trials that we experience on the earth plane are not experienced in other realms where total, unconditional love is the only energy, which resonates to higher evolvement. When people can grasp an understanding of the spirit world, they may realize that our loved ones can be and are closer than they were, even on the physical plane. Sure, we can grieve because we miss them, but we should be honest and acknowledge it for what it is—we miss them. It is our loss of them, not theirs of us, and in channelling, one can receive a greater understanding of people who have passed over and their inability to contact us, to let us know that they are in fact so close; and that they understand and see more than we can. Don't wallow in grief, for they are certainly not lost. Speak out your feelings and know that they will hear and understand how much you love them, even if it was hard to show them during their lives on earth. Know and understand that they love, accept, and understand you, for they are in a world that consists only of unconditional love, and anything other than love is not real.

This life we are living now, is the illusion people speak of, that anything exists outside of truth, love and God. The illusion is what we perceive as hardship, tests, trials; the feeling of being separate, separated from God. The reality where there is Truth, Love and God; is when one has come to the realization that only Love and God which in Truth are One, is real. The story or the struggle of life is an illusion we have created to feel separated, to experience life, separated from God, where our lives take on an adventure to find God, Peace and Oneness, which in fact is Truth or God. In fact, God, has never left us; for God is the Light, the intelligence within each atom or molecule of existence. In fact only God is real.

If you wish to forgive your loved ones, then do so and forgive yourself at the same time; they forgive you. If you need forgiveness, know that it is done and the need is no longer. Forgive yourself, and celebrate in the experience. If you are lost, then find yourself, for you are not that other person, the person who seems confused, separate from God; and that other person will never be and was never you. Find yourself, the self knowing and loving, by looking within and become a whole and beautiful creation. Know that God created you to live the gift of life and love. Know that these words are truth or step into the world of meditation and channelling and experience this and so much more for yourself. These truths have been handed down for centuries, but it is sometimes hard to believe them when there is no evidence, until you experience them for yourself. Know that the reason we can't identify with spirit, as the spirit world really is, is so that we can experience life in this realm, and as we live this life, and as we learn, we evolve. The more we evolve with light and truth, the greater our beings become. Know that what you see in this physical dimension is not the entirety of your being; it is only an aspect of a greater being, experiencing the gift of this life in this dimension.

The purpose for channelling is to bring Truth and Light into a world of illusion, deception and darkness. The illusion causes us to not remember who we are, so we believe parents, friends, teachers, partners, and anyone who will give us an identity. We try to live up to others' expectations and desires without going within and asking ourselves that all-important question that just about every soul who walks in this third dimension wishes to have answered; *"Who am I?"* Then we begin to deceive even ourselves, trying to fullfil a role that may not have been meant for us, being someone that we don't know and this is why so often our lives feel lost and as though we are wandering around in a dark fog. When a problem is solved, we feel lighter, less burdened and clear. This is what Truth can do for each and every one of us. We can turn our worlds around, uplift, heal and allow joy to be our light. The clearer and more advanced or more healed the channel is; the more light and truth will penetrate their consciousness. This is how we can connect with spirit. You will have to agree that Spirit is pure and like attracts like. The clearer and more healed you are as a medium the higher the energies that you as a medium will be able to contact and merge with. Remember Truth is pure and its essence is God and this is exactly what we are aiming to achieve, Truth and God or what is known as Self-Realization. As we heal ourselves, our minds and perceptions, more light enters into each cell and light is a vibration, so as we heal our vibration raises. This is why we go through processes of enlightenment, in order to clear the lower self and mind of misperceptions and untruths and heighten our own vibration, which enables beings of a higher vibration to work with and through us to bring greater truths and understandings to the earth plane. People of a higher vibration are nice to be around, you can feel their ambience, you can feel uplifted and healing can and does actually take place, just by being in the presence of an evolved channel. This is how Jesus, Buddha and great healers and teachers can and do heal.

My hope is that I have given you the reader, information that may uplift and enlighten, or at least help to make you a little more aware. I hope you begin to ask yourself some questions to help you remember that you are never alone, spirit is always right there to help and to guide you, to listen and to give guidance and understanding even when all feels totally lost, spirit is there. All that you need do is ask. Ask for a sign, a message or even a miracle. But remember to be open to receive what you ask for and also remember that what comes from spirit is the best for you at that time. *"Thy will be done"* not yours, because spirit and God can see and know the bigger picture of our life's journey and what we have asked to achieve in this life. Sometimes, what we want and ask for comes, not necessarily in the form that we think we want. Always accept with gratitude and grace and know that the divine plan is unfolding for our greatest good. Be open to the belief that what is unfolding in our lives at any time may be greater than even we can imagine at this time. This is where we learn about Trust and Faith. Have faith that Spirit and God are working for our good and trust that in time all will be revealed. See God as our loving father, overseeing our life as it unfolds, hesitant to intervene unless we look like we may really hurt ourselves. Always ready to offer advice and wisdom but do we choose to hear or do we think we know better as a child does.

Know that you can channel information from the highest of realms, from spirit and spirit guides, angels, masters or even God, or whatever you believe God to be. All we need do is ask and be open to receive. Clear yourself of old patterns and thought forms and be open to Channel. The reality of Spirit, and other dimensions is so beautiful, perhaps even beyond our imagination. Why not enter into the path of Meditation, Channel and ecstasy. One leads to the other. The process of Channelling reveals so many truths, and denies our ego of all its fantasy. Experience Love in its most divine form and become a radiant channel to the universe.

I would like to add and acknowledge at this point that the information, insights and writings in this book were mostly channelled from my beloved guides (in particlur, The Lady of the Golden Rose) and light beings that help me through all my trials and tribulations, who see me through my weaker moments when I momentarily forget. Thankfully they have and practice great patience, tolerance and understanding. The love I feel when communicating with them far transcends all other love and feelings of any human nature. I take this opportunity to give thanks to all of my beloved spirit friends and helpers for their unfailing support and for everything that they have helped me to create and understand. Love you guys.

Truth

*T*ruth as we know it is not necessary the Truth that is. Our Truth may shift and change. However it is important to grasp, speak and live our Truth as we perceive it. Then we may become strong in ourselves so that when Truth as it is, appears and we are ready and able to comprehend the Truth. Gradually we will believe and teach Truth as it is. Our Truth may change through many transformations throughout our Lives, always raising our consciousness and vibration.

Whilst preparing ourselves and our consciousness and our vibration, we grow and learn through many transformations. The ultimate goal is to be at one with the Truth, The I Am, The Source energy, The God Mind and illuminate peace and love. By this time, many lessons have indeed transpired and the only way to pierce the veil of self-deception, is to be hand in hand with God. And from this day—Judith—My precious Child you shall walk with thee, hand in hand and as you have fared the many challenges bravely and conquered all the dark side, and bathed and believed solely in the light—so shall the journey not falter here, but to continue on.

Your search as it were may be seen as the search for the Promised Land. Know and trust in your heart that the Promised Land wasn't some scoured out desert, in a forbidden land, centuries ago, but the desert you have journeyed through was indeed the way to the sacred garden. This Garden is filled with beauty and your beauty will magnify this beauty with an unlimited bright golden light that shines with the Glory of God. Than more to you will be attracted, like moths to the light on a dark night.

Stand and walk tall, speak and utter one sigh. The murmur of Love speaks through you and that murmur of Love shall enhance the hearts of many.

Beloved, Know and Trust and remain as always, a unique Child of the Universe, and beauty and light and love shall dwell within until the timeless days retire and the sun sets and rises no more, Beloved know and trust that you are loved.

I Hear the Beat

I hear the beat of a far away drum
My heart yearns for a distant place
A place little known to those who I am with
A place so long forgotten
A place where my family comes close
A place where people respect each other
And honour those that have come before them
A place so far in time and space
So few can ever remember that place
When peace held its reign in a mighty stance
This place was once my home

I feel so alone, for my people have gone
From a land that was my home
My people were destroyed by the White Man's Race
In a time when we shared the Spirit of Peace
And greed and egos were of little known
And anything bad was of disgrace
And faced with shame
This place was once my home

Lead by greed and an evil mind
The White Man came into my land
And took what was not ours to give
Nor to be taken from that place
Now that the time drawers near
When I shall see that day of grace
When the land shall be freed from that greedy race

This place was once my home
I have returned from that distant land
To awaken to Truth those of my race
And their minds and their hearts that have fallen prey
And fallen from that state of grace
To those that have slain for greed's sake
And slaughtered for a hungry pride
That seeks to take what even is mine
This place was once my home

To those who have destroyed my people and their land
Take note, Our Spirit of Our land
Will rise once again
Like the Phoenix from its ashes
And from whence it came
For I have returned not for vengeance sake
But to restore through justice what is mine
And to the Spirit of our Beloved Land
This place was once my home

One day I too shall fall from this place
I shall be asked from my fathers' face
I shall reply from a place of great peace
The land is free and once again in a state of grace
And can be enjoyed once again
My people shall return and work the land
The dream of peace and freedom will rule once again
And the White Man's race will be forgotten for all times sake
This place was once my home

And that beat of that special drum
That seems so near and so far away
That drum will return unto my ear
That drum shall beat with a freshness and rhythm
A rhyme of yesteryear
Then my soul can rest in peace
And I shall return but naught once again
To that Promised Land

This place is now my home

White feather is my name.

My Prison

The prison is within my mind.
The four walls of captivity is the sum total of being unaware.
Not being aware that we can live within our hearts.
That the heart can dissolve all the barriers of pain and fear,
Break down the toughest of fortresses.
We build fortresses, walls and barriers and prisons,
Within our minds, to keep the pain locked in.
We close our hearts off, to keep the people,
the friends and the healing out.
We can even build a void or a moat and surround ourselves and make
it the deepest and widest so that no one can get through.
We can live and dwell in isolation, in fear and anxiety.
Our minds can do that for us, so that no onslaught of laughter, or
frivolity, or tears can break through the veil of remorse.
The remorse is of circumstances, time, events and people that have
been, that cannot be changed.
The experiences that haven't gone the way we desired them to, maybe
someone's free will, free choice wasn't interested in being
entrapped in another's prison walls.
So the creator wore them, themselves.
No matter what, whatever we do, whatever we think, however we feel
and whatever we say, we need to be certain that we are creating, the
energy that we are putting out, is what we want to experience.
Because this is the truth, that everyone creates every feeling, every
thought, every word, and every action. What we put out there in our
reality, comes back to the creator to experience, multiplied.

If you experience joy, then joy will spread, and you will be
creating and manifesting joy.
If pain, or greed, or jealousy is experienced,
you will create more, until you become aware.
Once you have become aware, you can see the darkness you are
creating, then you can rise above it, into the light, then you can let it go,
the pain, being the victim, disappointments, sadness or grief. You can
rise above it, heal or transform your attitude, your perceptions, your
understanding, your experience of everything, can be a gift of light.

Accusations

as anyone ever been falsely accused, been judged, found guilty and punished and been innocent? Probably at one time or another we all have, whether it was a small thing or something shatters our life, or even destroys our reputation as we know it. It doesn't matter how small or big the accusation, what hits home or eats away at us; is the injustice. Maybe, that people didn't believe us, that they didn't trust us, that they didn't give us a chance to explain our perspective or even sometimes, it seems to be a vindictive lie about us. Then to be tried and found guilty, having neither been in the position to be able to prove your innocence nor having the opportunity to redeem your self-respect is daunting. I want you to think of a time, and I know everybody must have had at least one time, when they have been innocent and accused of being or doing something they have not done. Or perhaps you are not completely innocent, but things have been taken out of context and used against you for someone else's gain. For instance, let's look at Jesus. He didn't say; *"He was King on this Earth."* Jesus said in John 18:36; *"My Kingdom is not of this world: but now is my kingdom not from hence.:"* He meant the spirit world, or in my view the real world, but; noting that:—he was eventually crucified for this statement.

I would like you to feel just for a moment, how it felt to have been falsely accused, and how it felt to have to go through the punishment and degradation for something, which you either didn't do nor had any control over. How many of you believed, in your hearts, that one day the truth would come out and you would be vindicated, then your respect, your self esteem, would be resurrected and your pain and suffering and embarrassment would be annihilated. You would be found to be innocent or that it didn't matter because you were innocent anyway.

Then comes the test, did we forgive as Jesus did? *"Father, Forgive them; for they know not what they do."* Luke 23:34. Or did we hold on to the injustice and need to get even, to make them pay the debt. This is a test of faith and trust and of Love. We need to forgive them as Jesus did; or else it will hold onto us and pull us down until we do. Jesus was crucified on a cross and punished, for something he was not guilty of, and he prayed that God would forgive them, for their ignorance. He came here to teach us forgiveness and show compassion, he was and still is the example. The Lord's Prayer states: *"Forgive those who trespass against us"*.

Look deep within your heart and find the compassion, and forgive all those who have wronged you and search your minds and your souls for understanding. Jesus came here to show us the way to the Kingdom of Heaven. We have come to this earth as Jesus did; we are all too often accused of things we are innocent of, as was Jesus. Ask yourself this question, *"Can you forgive all those who have wronged you as Jesus did and love them as you love yourself?"*

If you can and try to live as Jesus did and taught us, and take him into our hearts, and trust in the divine plan, then he will indeed lead us into the Kingdom of Heaven.

The Truth is that while we hold on to accusations, hurts and pain, that this will keep us entrapped into the past. We are burdened by past resentments that eat away at our hearts, and cause continued stress. How can we forgive and let go of old torments that seem to replay like old broken records? The answer is simple, and the reason that Jesus came to this earth. The answer is to love; yes, through unconditional love. Love will set you free. Free the old, free the past, the hurt the pain and the sorrow by loving. Love yourself enough to break through all resentments once and for all time. Be free to love, live and enjoy. We can hold on and be entrapped by the past pain and resentment or, we can let go and be free to love, laugh and dance in the Light of Forgiveness. Be free and Love.

If we were to hold on to the pain, the resentment, be aware it will eat away at you and cause discomfort, or even disease. Louise Hay wrote a book, *"You can Heal your Life,"* a book of affirmations to release the causes to diseases and illness caused from blockages such as resentment, torment, grudges, guilt or anxiety. When circumstance seem to betray you, and you feel the injustice of criticism and ignorance, release yourself from the tensions and move into your heart and forgive them for their ignorance and forgive and love yourself and be free.

Betrayal

O f all the lessons and hardships we as humans are required to experience, betrayal somehow leaves the most bitter of taste, in one's mouth or stomach. When those that you have loved, honored, trusted, respected and even defended and supported and confided in, find the necessity to sink the knife of betrayal, spite and vindictiveness in you; can become a very dark night for your Soul. Usually for some trivial egotistic pursuit, which more often than not leaves them abandoned and in more trouble than they can handle. For you cannot take something and keep it, if it is not rightfully yours, and whatever is rightfully yours will somehow find a way of returning, possibly in an equal or even greater form. For instance, if someone steals your beloved from you, then they were not really with you, and they will either return with commitment and a greater love and loyalty, or someone who can love you more will be there for you. When, for whatever reason you need to experience this particular lesson, or someone finds a need to take from you something that is not rightfully theirs to take, one needs to build a bridge of understanding and healing over the void that their loss seems to leave behind. This sometimes is the hardest of acts of love we need to practice, but in the long run is one of our greatest opportunities of growth.

Can we forgive, love and find empathy and compassion for those that make the most vicious attack of all? Those people we love and accept and share with, then turn on us and attack us from within the boundaries of our own hearts. Our defences are weak, our beliefs are tested, our faith can be shaken or even destroyed, our love and hearts can be shattered and our souls can become fractured and fragmented in disbelief, uncertainty and discouragement. The grief can be overwhelming, and the test to stay true, centred and in love is sometimes too great and unbearable. We find ourselves tortured and may even decline into depression.

We are then asked for nothing less than to love our brother one hundred percent. Trust our brothers and accept them for who they are. Then they turn the sword of vengeance, deceit and betrayal and twist it through our hearts, until we bleed so much that our reality is torn from its shaky foundations, and we tremble as we begin to restructure our reality and belief system, based on Truth, honesty and integrity.

Betrayal in all her mighty guises hits all of us at some stage of our development, quite often with repeat experiences. More often than not when we are weary and think that we have finally achieved success, a task or goal or even a new understanding and realization. We may think that we are finally getting somewhere and are successful and then like thunder, the self created illusion is shattered and your heart is stripped of its joy and we sink into the depths of despair and disillusionment, in one fowl sweep of the sword of betrayal. We fall down to our knees and cry out, *"why?"*

The task is to begin to climb out of what for some is a dark hole or, dark night of the soul', as it has come to be known, and begin to piece together the fractured and scattered parts of our world. We need to heal the hole where the hunk of illusion was torn away, for if it were truth, if it were real, it would have sustained. Nothing can hurt you if you stand in the light of truth. If it hurts, than let it go and allow a new understanding and perspective to be brought forward. In truth, that person has done you a great service in denying your falseness anymore, and they have helped to peel away another layer of deception and illusion. The belief that we were anyone or that we had anything to take was in truth false. And when we rise up and look face to face into the eyes of God, the light pierces the veil of self-deception. Once again, we begin to understand in all humility that nothing has been taken away except a load to heavy to bear any further, compiled of falseness and ego. Attempts at believing, that we were or had something that never really existed except in the imaginings of our own minds. And we come to a deeper understanding about the frailty of the human ego.

Thank the perpetrator for the justice in this hideous act and smile from within. Then when you suddenly discover the service they have rendered unto you by dislodging the irons that have bound you and kept you prisoner in an illusion of needing or having to be something or someone, which you weren't. Now you are free, now you can choose to be who you really are or want to be. Now that this particular pattern of behaviour or belief system has been shattered, you can now restructure your life with a new foundation, based on truth from your higher self or even God. You can rest in knowing that you will never need to deal with that particular lesson again. If you have grown in awareness somewhat, you may be able to apply it to other structures and patterning and transform them as well and save even greater pain later.

Your light shines brighter and lighter than ever before and you bask in the knowledge that you have taken a giant step forward in humility. The falseness subsides and the strength and beauty of truth shines forth once again. One very large step closer to our all-enhancing goal of oneness with self and the creator has been accomplished.

That which you are not has served its purpose in protecting you from the light of truth for a period until you grew through your restrictions and limitations and were freed to be you, to dare to be vulnerable and whole and stand in your own glory of humility. And even this too shall come to pass!

What of the perpetrator, who through patterns of fear, jealousy and envy have dislodged a part of what is in fact, false? They will not only have to bear the weight and the torment of being something they were not, but also they have reaped the token of karma. That which you do to others will be done unto you.

The test: If someone asks you for your coat, then give it and if you have another give it too. If someone slaps your cheek, turn the other to be slapped as well. Then love them and praise them for their kindness, for when you stand in all truth and in all humility, nothing will be standing other than the Christ which is you less your ego and which has laid dormant in some for decades, lifetimes and possibly eons of time. And when the Christ stands before you, kneel in love and ask forgiveness for your sins and repent for all time. Thy will be done and no amount of egotistical power or force will ever triumph over the hand of Truth and Justice which brings balance to our frayed egos and corrupt minds when we fall from Grace to journey once again, through the illusion of pain and suffering.

Love those that would take from you, yield your pittance of mortal ego so that you are stripped of everything false and immortality glows brighter.

Let go and let God, let go of everything that can be taken from you, so that you can stand in Grace and nothing can be taken from you again. And that once bitter taste of remorse can be dissolved into the sweetness of understanding, and the knowledge that those who would take from you and give false testimony will be equally plucked from their egotistic demise of falseness and self-deception.

When you restructure your life and yourself, build with honour and integrity and understand that as you create, you will experience; and dance in the supreme knowledge that you have indeed experienced the gift of life in all of its Glory.

Pain and Sorrow

*P*ain equals resistance, which causes sorrow. It is that simple, but the cure is not so easy. Physical pain is the body resisting disease and even death. If you are in pain, ask and look at what you are resisting. For instance, if you get a headache, you may need water, sleep, or to sort things out. Pain is the body's way of telling you something is not right and you need to correct it. Many forms of physical pain and illness are brought about by the emotional state of being, usually being in denial and resisting to see things in another context or from a different perspective, or indeed from another's point of view.

Emotional Pain is brought about by resisting, usually resisting to let-go, and holding on causes the emotional trauma, heartache and pain that we endure in the hope to hold on to a particular belief pattern or person or object of desire. Remember every soul has a journey, a path that they can learn and grow from. It is their gift, their right to be able to experience and play in life. It is when we are attached, dependent and co-dependent which causes pain. It can be that we are resisting our own path, our own journey and experience, or it can even be that we are trying to control or manipulate another person's choices, maybe even someone they love. We resist our own path because we are afraid of being alone, and yet aloneness is the essence of freedom. You can be in a room or even a city for that matter, filled with people and be the loneliest person in the universe. This is when you need to stop and realize that you are dependent on someone else to make you happy, or less bored. When you are in that state of being, when that person you long to be with, eventually shows up, more often than not, you will have a disagreement or argument with them. This is because, you are not fulfilled and in balance and in harmony with yourself. There is something within you that you don't like going on. You are angry and need someone else to take it out on instead of accepting responsibility and looking at what is going on inside of you. Usually, when this happens you don't like yourself, or some part of yourself, and resist looking at such issues. You don't feel whole or complete with yourself and want some other person to fill the gap or void in your life. You are resisting the opportunity to deal with what is holding you back from fulfilling yourself or your life. From my observation, most pain is related to people leaving people or not leaving, whichever is present, which comes down to resisting freedom and letting go of someone. If you are in a relationship and your partner moves on or leaves for whatever reason, let them go. Allow them the space and freedom to grow and to experience their life's lessons, life and everything else. If you say, *"I still love them"*, then love them and let them go, if they love you or they are meant to be with you, they will return. If you resist which is what most people do and is the cause of pain, you will create more pain, which will lead to anxiety and eventually, illness, which causes more pain. If you are stuck in a relationship and the other person won't go, then you are resisting stepping into your own power and releasing them or taking the steps necessary to bring about your freedom. Opportunity is knocking for you to become empowered and you are resisting because of fear of being alone.

Many people have a fear of being alone, or by themselves. We can hold onto the security of having someone else help you to make the decisions that really are your responsibility. Holding on to a partner or a child may be your way of hiding from taking your responsibility to live life, or the security of having someone to take that responsibility for you. Many of us hide in fear of being left behind, of having to face ourselves and to take responsibility for ourselves. Sometimes our own company is too much too bare. And it is in those instances that we must truly look within and do the inner work, to help us to progress to a stage of development when we must take our responsibility and cherish who we are so that we enjoy our own companionship, for if we do not like ourselves, why should we expect anyone else to?

And of course when someone dies, we all feel sad. Feel your sadness and your grief and allow the grieving process to take place, but understand you are grieving because you miss them, not because of their loss—but yours. The longer you hold on, the more pain you will experience. Love them and let them go on with their journey. They have completed their part of this journey and now need to go onto the next stage of their development, which also gives you the opportunity to move onto your next part of your journey. If you truly love them, you will always be with them in spirit. It is good to note here that every failure or loss is an opportunity to experience freedom, and every success is a stepping-stone to something more or greater.

Mental pain comes in many forms also, such as frustration, anger, depression, anxiety, which all lead to one kind of illness or another. This pain also more often than not stems from emotional upheavals and traumas. In all the cases I can think of, the remedy is to let go. Even simple disappointments, can be cured by letting go of the attachment to outcomes that are not meant to be. If something doesn't happen the way you would like at any given time, it doesn't mean that it won't at another time or in another situation. But it also means, you are not ready for that experience, or there is still something more or something else that is required of you before that desire can be fulfilled. The simplest thing to do is to let go of the desire, and stop resisting the opportunity that is being offered to you, and allow God or the universe to bring about your desires. When you are ready for that experience, we will need to look at Trust. Usually, what is in front of us turns out to be even better than what we wanted anyway. For instance, we can use an analogy like this one; if we were to want a Rolls Royce and can only afford the Toyota, you probably are not ready to deal with the social challenges related to owning a Rolls Royce. Your friends may decide that you have outclassed them, and accuse you of being a snob etc. This behaviour is not spiritually correct, but still does exist. You may not be ready to let go of your existing friends and become acquainted with being socially accepted by the, 'Rolls Royce's class of people', but when you are able to step up, you will be able to afford to own a Rolls Royce, and afford the maintenance and insurance and all the extra demands that goes with owning a Rolls Royce.

The bottom line is if you are experiencing pain in some form or another, you are resisting, or holding on and resisting letting go and moving on. Holding on can also cause pain for the other person. Have you ever felt squeezed? Let go and let God bring about your desires. Trust in God, your higher self and the Universe, then they all know what they are doing and allow your life to unfold lovingly and with ease. Letting go does not mean you don't love someone or something. Quite the contrary, it means you love them enough to allow them their life, their freedom, you can love them anyway and when they are ready, they will be there for you, or you will both move on to a greater understanding and experience of love.

Faith 'I Surrender to the Bigger Picture'

With faith I keep moving on, it's known as Faith in the future. Sometimes in life the only thing we have left which is truly our own is faith. Sometimes, very often, my faith in other people and myself is let down, but the faith I have in God and Spirit always caries me over my depths of despair. There was a time when I had everything in my life that I could possibly want and ask for, except myself. I lived in a world of illusion and deceit, mostly deceiving myself and pretending to be happy. As with all illusion and lies, this had to fall apart. And faith will see me to creating something even greater than before, this time on the solid foundation of Truth and this time with myself, conscious and whole. A vision I have had is to help people find their faith, their peace of mind and love. I asked my guides, God, *"Can you help me to help others?"* I was told to Trust. To Trust in myself and in my Faith. Know that I am a part of the bigger picture. We need many small dots to create the whole picture. And I am a dot or more to the point, a light in the bigger scheme of things to take place, to join with other lights or dots to form a huge bright light or picture.

I asked my higher self to show me the way to be whole in myself and if each small dot or light strives to be whole and brighten their light within themselves, we can create the greatest picture of all time.

'I am whole, I am one with the universe.'

This wholeness comes through having and trusting in faith, that my part, my path, is designed especially for me. I have faith that the hardships endured have made me a stronger, more determined person, more willing to succeed, more appreciative of my gifts and talents and all in all, a more whole and more creative person. Life is a wonderful gift, if we can just trust and surrender to faith. Acknowledge that God created the entire universe in every small and finite detail. Understand that we are a part of that universe, no matter how small a dot we are, understand that we have a place to fill and if we weren't here doing our bit and creating our part of the picture, the bigger picture would never be complete. It would be like a jigsaw puzzle with a piece missing.

Life is a wonderful gift if we can just trust and have faith that all is as it should be and be the best dot or light you can be and create the most beautiful picture of Peace and Harmony and Love you could ever imagine. Have Faith that if we do our bit, then God will do the rest.

Have Faith that you can trust that Spirit and God is in the drivers' seat and that you can let go and let God and be fully present to enjoy every moment of contentment, joy and harmony. Have an open heart and be open to every possibility for life to unfold into a beautiful cosmic experience. Have the Faith to trust, let go and let God bring about your desire.

Forgiving
Christmas is For Giving and Forgiving

s I drove my car on the lonely trip back from the Coast, with *'Amazing Grace'* and *'So This is Christmas'* alternating repeatedly in my mind, I stopped to think that to forgive is to give an awful lot of yourself.

To forgive, you need to give love, unconditional love and you are in full humility—your pride and your ego are sure to have endured a beating. You need to find courage to face perhaps defeat or even ridicule and pain even when you find in your heart the space for forgiving. You need strength to support your courage in case your love and humility are met with another even stronger onslaught of attack. You need self-esteem and self-love, in case your kindness and attempts at reconciliation meet with more ridicule, or abuse. You need understanding to acknowledge and accept that the person or the people are suffering from misconception, misunderstanding, guilt, anger or ignorance. You need Compassion, to love them and yourself with empathy, humility and understanding. You need Acceptance that you are you and they are wherever they are and may not be ready to accept any other point of view and may even refuse your forgiveness. When you forgive, you give of yourself, your energy, your love, and your soul. Hence the saying to forgive is divine.

These lessons have long plagued my being, causing pain, confusion, and heartache. When I was a child, I very quickly became aware of how sensitive I was. The sad part is that nobody else realized and understood and worse still is, that I didn't understand. I learnt that people quite often lashed out with the intent to take away my power, as a means to take away my authenticity and to control me, as people do. When people attack, they take from that person, and when they forgive, they give. Often attack comes from defence, guilt, selfishness and more often than not jealousy. Somebody has something that person doesn't have and they want it, or somebody wants to take something away from that person. My openness and sensitivity suffered greatly in my younger days as many people experience, believing there was something wrong with myself, my being. In this instance many retreat into themselves as I retreated over and over again to the world of spirit and nature spirits, fairies, angels and magick.*(I intentionally use the "magick" in this book instead of "magic" to distinguish from it ordinary "magic". The later is what illusionists use to perform and entertain an audience with whereas the former is derived from God and is spiritual based.)* The problem was that I was the only one who could see, hear or know this magick. I loved it and my family and friends thought crazy things because of my withdrawal and their ignorance. Even today, my family and friends of yesterday have no idea of my ability to connect to the spirit realms or of my world.

The rejections, aggressiveness, attacks, anger and frustration and ignorance bore heavily on my self-esteem and broke my heart and shattered my soul. Even today I am still very heavily tested with attacks of jealousy, slander and malignment. And it is only recently that I have come to understand completely how it is very much and totally the other person's problem. At last I can now see clearly, that people attack and take because they may feel threatened, inferior, incomplete, and jealous. And only now I don't allow them to take from my heart, spirit and soul. It is only now I have found the strength of love, compassion and understanding to withstand the great tests and in these times to give love, understanding and compassion. I am not saying that acts of betrayal, lies, ridicule, and vindictive gossip does not hurt, I am saying I don't allow them to take from me or destroy me anymore. I may retreat and search for what it is, what aspect of me is showing itself in the form of attack or abuse which wants to surface and be healed once and for all time. To resolve this issue is a great step forward and it will not be resolved until we can forgive it. This is what Jesus came here to teach us:—Love, to have compassion and to forgive.

Sometimes, to forgive is a very challenging process. Life is a process of experiencing, learning and evolving to greater heights, greater love and greater experiences.

Christmas can be the perfect time to forgive, the past events, to forgive the mistakes and misunderstandings of the people around you. Realize those people are doing a service to you, as I have finally come to discover and understand, that we are all one, we are all connected. You are an aspect of me; I am an aspect of you. If I see you as being beautiful, that is within me. If I see you as ugly, that is also a part of me who wishes to surface and be cleared. Look seriously at the people around you. See what attracts and what repulses you. They can be your greatest teachers, and this process can make you so much more aware.

One of my greatest teachers once said to me, *"See the beauty in everything"*. Now I understand that statement. For instance, if my weight stirs feelings or thoughts of rejection, uneasiness or even repulsion in you, you need to look at what part of your life you had a weight problem. Realize that your repulsion is a call for awareness for something in your life, which needs to be healed, released, and ultimately forgiven. If you see and are in awe of my spirituality, than that part of you also wishes to emerge and allowed to flourish. You can only see and relate to what is within yourself, and sometimes, these aspects come from so deep within, we wonder where it came from. At these times we need to be extremely honest with ourselves, and love ourselves even more.

Look around you, take notice of what you see in people and in situations and become aware of what aspect of yourself you are denying, not loving, not forgiving and thank that person or situation for bringing it to your attention. Understand and know that we are all one, each person, each situation is an opportunity to love yourself more and more.

The New Year will bring new situations, new people, a new cycle and new opportunity. How can you move into it and take advantage of the wonders and magic that are about you, to be bestowed upon you if you are loaded down with burdens, resentment, and the judgments of people and situations from the past, let them go, sort things out this week, and let them be gone, once and for all.

Christmas eve, prepare yourself, go to church, pray and ask for forgiveness and give thanks and heartfelt gratitude for all that you have received. Christmas Day is for giving, appreciating, loving and giving and forgiving, and only then does our world know and understand peace. You will become at peace and in harmony with the flow of life, in all its many paradigms.

Give your gifts of love, acceptance, understanding and forgiveness and enjoy the fruits of your harvest of the year to come.

Boxing Day is to package everything up and let them go and await the miracle of a New Year to follow.

May the Love of Christ be with you and bless you and may you find peace, love and forgiveness on the deepest level of your heart and soul.

Time

There is no time like the present

The present is with us now and forever

In the past we were at the present

And in the future we will be present

The past is not present

The future is not present

The only time present is "now"

Live now and be present

The journey is now and present

A gift to you is to enjoy the present.

Love is
Not the Answer

O h! What sacrilege—how dare this woman write such a statement that contradicts so many peoples' perceptions, teachings and beliefs? *"How dare she?"*

I dare because I hear so many people's stories—life tragedies and tales of deceit and betrayal. How many wars are waged in the name of love, either in homes, workplaces and relationships of all kinds? Battlefields are in all walks of life.

I say this because Love is a concept of duality. The opposite of Love is hatred—fear and entrapment. Where there can be an opposite, how can that be *Truth*? Because *Truth* sustains, *Truth* cannot be right today and wrong tomorrow. *Truth* is a constant. *Truth* is something that I can believe in and trust that it will be there when I need it the most. When everything else breaks down, I will still have my Truth, and it will see me through those dark days when I am lost and broken. When those that I Love and trust have let me down, and when I cannot see or feel—Love.

I tried Love—when it failed—it was my fault. It was not unconditional Love. I had conditions and expectations that lead me to disappointment and loneliness. I tried again to love in the face of attack; hatred; belittlement; insults; abuse, whether it be physical, mental or emotional. That is where my journey began, the journey to Love. I believed that Love was the answer. Through books, teachers, writings, songs, and poetry, I believed that Love was the answer. I believed if I could only find Love,

I would find fullfilment, happiness, peace and contentment. I would find Love and I would find God. I would find the answer to life and all it represented.

When I began, totally broken, disillusioned and in total agony, both inside and out—I asked, *"Where did I go wrong?"* My answer in truth was—*"You loved another more than yourself. You didn't Love yourself. You gave and gave until you had nothing left to give. You had expectations. You created this situation with your thoughts."*

For twelve years I devoted my life, my mind, my heart, my being to finding Love. Many times I thought yes; this time I've got it. This is it, this time I've found Love, only to get told by prophecy and others, you don't Love yourself. Love deeper—go deeper. Love yourself first and Love will overflow and everybody you touch will Love also. Love and they will be transformed or move away. I believed this. I taught this. I waged my reputation on Love.

Failure after failure—I moved into unconditional Love, loving people in spite of their defects, in spite of their jealousies, their selfishness. In spite of their greed—Love them anyway.

Then one day I sat down and I thought for a long time. I contemplated my life—and—this is what I did years ago. This is what led me to a total breakdown, loving others without anything in return, loving others without condition. This has been a merry-go-round. I am back where I began, only this time; I Love myself. This time I am aware. This time I am conscious, but why isn't it working? Why can't I find Love, acceptance, fulfillment? I asked God, *"Are you there? Do you exist? Aren't you Love? Where did I go wrong?"*

Then one day—I dare to go against all the teachings and beliefs and say Love is not the answer.

Love won't bring me joy—for what joy is there in receiving another's abuse and judgment. What joy is there in loving my bruises, whether they are physical, mental or emotional?

35

Love does not bring peace, for what peace is there in loving someone's ugliness, bad temper, bad morals, or loving your own beat-up brain. What peace is there when people wish to take from you, whatever they can get or hurt you so that they can vindicate their egos?

Love does not bring acceptance. You can accept everything and everyone, and every wrong that people can throw at you, but that does not make you accepted by others. You can accept yourself without being received and accepted by others. Just because others use you, or abuse you, does not make you accepted.

Love does not bring fulfillment. How fulfilled are you when your partner walks out of your life for another, even though you loved them. Even though you loved yourself and them equal. Even though they were seeing someone else and you loved them and everyone else too.

Love does not bring fulfillment even when you love someone as a friend. You enjoy their company to a degree. You overlook their obscenities for a period. You accept and acknowledge their love to you, but you can't feel that closeness that leads to intimacy with them. Even when you receive more love than you possibly feel you can give love, does not bring you that feeling of satisfaction, or fulfillment.

When we meet that special person, when everything is perfect, love, sex, intimacy, money, home, companionship, understanding, are you fulfilled when you fight or disagree about the garbage, the children, which holiday destination, bills being and not being paid? Is love there, when you feel more alone than when there was nobody there? Then; at least you had yourself.

Love is not there when I am broken, when I need love most. Love is there when I am in love. When I can enjoy the blue sky, smell the roses, watch the bird's fly and the butterflies, and the wind dance. But where is Love when my child dies? Where is Love when I lose everything I have? Where is Love when the person I Love, says; "I don't Love you anymore!" Where is Love when people or circumstances trash your dream, your beliefs, your reputation, and your peace of mind? Where did Love go?

It was only a moment ago when I was so totally in Love, It would last forever it would seem, or until disaster happens. Where did Love go when I lost myself?

Where is Love when you see children starving to death? Where is Love when you are so angry and hurt that you beat someone to a pulp? Where is Love when you are found guilty of a crime you did not do? Where is Love when your best friend cries out for help and you can't give it? If Love were real, if Love were Truth, wouldn't it be there?

If Love were Truth, then even though it may hide, Love would still come to the rescue. If Love were real, you wouldn't be able to lose it in the first place. If Love were true than why does one need to search their heart, the world, the inner worlds, the different realms, life, the universe to find it? If Love were true, why does Love need to hide? If Love were Truth, than why can't I see it, feel it and know it?

So, then I found Compassion. Compassion is so much Love, that you learn to love even your enemies. You may not like what they do, but you love them anyway. Compassion is the ultimate. But is it? Is it real? Is Compassion Truth? Can I count on compassion when everything else has failed?

Let's look at Compassion. Compassion is made up of Unconditional Love with understanding. Let's see—*"I don't agree with you bashing my children senseless, but I understand that you have had a dreadful child-hood, so I'll love you anyway."* It just doesn't cut it anymore. What about the senseless children? *"I hurt so much that I don't feel anymore. I am innocent, but I understand that you needed someone or something to take your frustration out on. I don't approve of your bashing me. I don't even like it, but I love you anyway."*

Do you want to laugh or do you want to cry or do you want to be sick at heart. This is not Love. This is not Truth. This is not the answer.

Love is not the answer.

I hear already someone saying, *"Judy, you've got it all wrong. You have misinterpreted the meaning of Love. This is not what Love is about."*

Isn't it? Then what is Love about? The reason my life was destroyed was because I didn't Love myself. Well, now I do Love myself and this world is still wrong. Love just doesn't cut it anymore. And if I have missed it or Love is hiding from me after a life time, then I don't want it anymore, because I can't count on it, I can't trust it.

I am human, I have feelings, I have a mind, and I have desires. If I have to deny them, then I should be a spirit. God gave me a body and all my senses to experience not only Love, but also hatred; to experience pain, fear and exhaustion—joy and happiness and peace. God or my parents, whatever you believe in, gave me a life and a body to be and to live and to appreciate and condemn and to laugh and to cry, to run and to walk, to build and to fall down, to think and to sleep and to dream; to experience life and existence, in all of its wonderment, and in all of its torment.

What sustains me, not Love, but the Breath? Without the Breath, I am nothing or I am Spirit. Without the Breath, I cease to exist as I am.

What makes me breathe? When I was a child I worked this one out. When life tormented me, I would hold my breath and wish and hope to cease to exist. I don't need to be on a respirator to appreciate my breath and to understand that the breath sustains me, that my breath is there when Love is gone or hiding.

What makes me Breath?	Consciousness.
What is consciousness?	Life—or maybe even God.
Who makes me breath?	Myself.
Who am I?	Consciousness.
What is consciousness?	God.

Who made the air that I breathe? What is the air? What is Love? What is Compassion? What are Joy and peace and fulfillment?

It is God. Love is even God. And what are pain and fear and agony and terror and trauma? This is also Life and yes, also God—but not Love.

Love is not the answer. To ascend to a space of existence with joy and appreciation of Life and God and everything, we need to touch into a space of what some may call Grace.

Not with Love, but with the Grace of God, I shall accept and endure all things. Jesus said, "I am the way." Not the answer.

Jesus said, *"Love thy neighbor as thyself."* Not that Love is the answer. Where is this way taking us too; to seek out and understand God? To know God is to know Love and Truth, but Love by itself is not the all. We also need to learn Discernment, Compassion, Understanding, Acceptance and Unconditional Love.

Love yourself first and, yes! Then you can Love others unconditionally, but be aware that life is full of lessons, obstacles and challenges and without these, we would not appreciate the miracles, the joy and the laughter.

See each experience in Love and ask the Grace of God to be with you always. See the Light in everyone's eyes and know that somewhere God is hiding behind that smile or that tear. But believe me—I may always see and feel God, but sometimes I don't see or feel Love. God is the answer.

But this is me and this is also my Truth.

So I read my article out to my congregation, my masterpiece, my Truth and I received the mixed reactions that I had anticipated; and now I ask, *"What now? Lord?"* Some agreed whole-heartedly with the article. It touched some so deeply, they don't even know how or why and some people just put up their blocks. I don't agree! This is not possibly true; it comes from a bitter and twisted experience that will in time fade, and Judy will return to her former understandings and beliefs, nice and simple teachings that resonate to our belief patterning, that don't rattle our self induced cages, when she grows some more, she will see the error of her ways. *"Were you to run with this article Judy, it would destroy you. Remember Jesus, he was crucified for speaking out Truth that was not what everyone wanted to hear".*

I guess my purpose is to help people to awaken in whatever way my guides see fit, because suddenly, Truth seems far more important than Love. Not Love on a God level or higher planes, but Love as most people on Earth see it. My Life has been extremely challenging and because of my stubbornness, I refused for years to admit and to see, never mind understand that when we humans can see, feel and know Love, there can be hatred, disillusionment, and disappointment.

I believed whole-heatedly that when we reached Love, when we could Love regardless of desire, we would be there. There would be nowhere else to go. Now I realize, we can even Love and hate at the very same time. We can love the person and hate how they treat us all at once.

This is my awakening that life has many twists and turns at every corner. What does all this mean, now? Where am I now; that my beliefs and faith and truth have altered so much? What does it mean to my life that I have been lead to a point on the highest peak to find that it was all an illusion after all? The struggle to stay in love, to love no matter what is to deny my own truths, my own feelings—believing that what I was feeling, seeing was not real; struggling to keep my lie alive, to hold onto my belief, that when I did find Love; everything would fall into place. I would be whole and purposeful and fulfilled. Now I am aware that it is all up to me. I am the only one who can make a difference in my world. I can love the people in this world but hate some of the things that they do to others and it is okay to feel this way and admit that there are other emotions that override love at times.

Instead of running around trying to find someone else to love me, and then being disillusioned or broken when they don't do it the way that I want to be loved. Finally the Light strikes like thunder, it is all up to me, and no one else can do it for me, even if I let them. It is always up to me, always has been and always will be; me! It is my choice, and nobody can choose for me.

I am the only one that can Love me and nurture me—the way I need to be loved and nurtured. I can share this love, but I can't give it to someone else nor receive it from someone else. They have their own type of love that they need. I am the love that loves through me and that is probably the best it will ever be. To be the love, not feel it, but be it, don't try to do it, be it—Be Love in all of its wonderment and in all of its mystery, be loving in everything you do and are.

Love yourself and be yourself, whatever that is at the time. As long as I can still touch into that space in the centre, detach from what is happening and move into the space in which I can love myself, I can find peace. I can then surrender to whatever is going on in the outside world and know that I can find love, love of self within. I can take this love out into the world and try to share this love with those around me. All I have to do is to remember who I am and that I am loving myself, that I am not what is happening, I am not the experience, I am not the other person, I am me.

Eternal Love

The more I love the more love there is to love with. The eye above the crown, symbolizes God is watching me and watching over me. Which in turn says,' The Love of God is within me, and this angel of love, brings love and shares love with all those around me.

Stillness

Listen to me tell you a story.
When I was so young many lifetimes ago
I met a young man standing ever so still
I asked him why he stood so still
He replied, *"I am still because of time*
I am still because of love
I am still because of pain and sorrow"
I asked him again, *"But why are you still?"*
He replied, *"There is no time, no space*
There is no pain, no sorrow. There just is!
And to be able to recognize
That these things are not what they seem
You need to stay in a state of stillness
Stillness will bring an appreciation of what really is"
I asked, *"what really is?"*
He replied, *"There is stillness, there is love, there is consciousness*
There is being, just being"
The young man said, *"There is nothing else, nothing else matters*
When the world comes to realize this, then and only then
Will there be unconditional Love
Then there will be one, and only one
Then there will be stillness
That day will come and we will be free!"

You Can't Fail

*I*t has finally dawned on me, as I face making life changing decisions, I look at what is in front of me and I am aware of so many choices. As the old fear wants to raise its ugly head and say, *"But what if you make the wrong choice, what if you fail?"* It's almost enough to think, 'Well, maybe I shouldn't do anything,' at least where I am, and with what I am doing, I am surviving. Life continues and after all is said and done; I am very comfortable with where I am now. Life is very good to me at the moment. But why have I undergone so many lessons, and learnt so much? Why have I had to struggle so hard, just to be here?

No, I know I have come this far for something more. I've been having a rest, and recuperating—re-charging my batteries, not just to sit on this mountaintop and enjoy the view, although if I could, that would be very pleasant for a while, anyway.

But I know something deep inside of me is stirring; something is taking place. Plans are formulating. The voice says, *"It's time to put what you have learnt into practice. Trust it, know it and be it."* Notice I said, 'be it' and not, 'do it,' a subtle difference that has taken many disappointments and seeming failures, hurts, and much disillusionment to understand the difference. Doing is a state of control, stemming from a desire of the ego or mind to accomplish something. Being is a state of existence that takes place from your essence, from your knowing. I don't believe I am feminine, I know I am feminine. A subtle difference, but one of the most profound acknowledgements you can have. I don't believe I love you, I know I love you. I am not doing love, I am being love.

I look at my many choices, decisions to make and also seeing the possible setbacks and I anticipate problems that will undoubtedly appear. I look at what I might gain and possible losses. My imagination at this stage is rampant with all kinds of possibilities and I can create many pictures and scenarios of possible future outcomes.

One thing I have learned through my life experiences that appeared to be failures, is that I have no control over what happens, what people do or say and sometimes even though I know better, it seems like even over my own actions and reactions and responses, and especially my emotions. I know in my heart that this is not true. I can control what I say, what I do, what I think and even what I feel. I am the creator of my own destiny. I've learnt in the many workshops and seminars, know what the goal is, see the goal, feel the goal, breathe the goal in and charge toward it and don't stop until you reach it. Whatever happens, don't lose sight of that goal.

However, I have thought I have failed so many times, I never reached the goal, and when I did persevere through whatever the universe threw my way to prevent me from obtaining my desire at that time, I discovered that I didn't really want it anymore. Getting back to the question, what is the answer, it is simple, "I surrender. I surrender to that force that pushes and pulls me. That divine force that some may call all kinds of names, such as my higher self, Spirit, Guides, and guardian angels, God, the Universe, luck or even fortune, or fate. I simply surrender and be who I am at this time. Do the things that I need to do, make the best decisions in the moment and simply be the best that I can be.

How can I fail? There is no such thing as failure. We live for eternity, we incarnate into the physical realm to experience life, to learn, to teach, to understand and to experience life to the fullest, and just be. How can we fail? Every breath we take is a success and every opportunity is a miracle just waiting to happen, and every accomplishment is a joy.

I cannot fail to be, and by simply taking advantage of opportunities is a success, as long as I don't let my mind interfere. As long as I remember who I am, and what my essence is, and respond and react accordingly in love and from love. I cannot fail; there is no such thing as failure, just another opportunity to experience and enjoy.

Afraid to Love

After a very intense soul awakening, intense and powerful situations arising and exploding before and around me, whilst soul searching and going deeper and deeper than ever before. The answer was being thrown in my face repeatedly, in true-life situations and reflected in movies and theatre.

After much consideration, I have come to the conclusion, that if we wish to experience healing; for the world to heal, we need to love. When we are in love, the world will mirror love. If the world mirrors love for a short time, understand that we have touched love. The longer the world reflects love, the deeper we are in love. Become transparent and fall totally in love, become love and watch the world heal and become love.

You may be saying 'who or what do I love', and I will say unto you, "love—love your life, the sun rising in the morning, the sound of rain on the roof, love the trees, the flowers, your pets, your friends, your family, love until all you can see is love." And you may say, 'what is Love', and I will say, "Love is God, Love is you, Love is me, Love is everything and everyone. Love is the energy or the vibration that everything good is created from." You see Love is energy so powerful that it can heal, it can dissolve hatred and fear, and it can make the world a heaven, a place of tranquillity and harmony and peace.

You may say to me, 'I have loved, but I don't see what you speak of.' And I will say, *"You don't love enough, you don't love unconditionally, you don't love without expectation. You are afraid to Love totally and fully because you may get hurt"*. Most people only love if they are loved in return and as much as they are loved, that is until they have children. Then they learn to love unconditionally, then they love their baby totally, no bars held, then they love completely and once you have had that beautiful little baby and you love it totally, unconditionally and with all your heart, you see that love being returned as the child grows and the smiles melt your heart into the oneness. This is total love, you the adoring parent, the baby smiling with love and God.

And I will say unto you, *"Love!—Love unconditionally, without condition or expectation, without wanting anything and you will never be hurt."* You may say, 'how do I know when I am loving everyone enough?' And I will say unto you, *"Look at what is before you. If you can see love, then you are loving enough, and if you don't then love more deeply."* And I will say unto you "Are you trying to give it away, why don't you love yourself first? Love yourself, nurture yourself and watch your cup overflow and flow onto others and watch the magic energy flow onto everyone and everything and watch as it transforms the negative into positive. Watch as it turns wrongful situations into peaceful and harmonious times. Watch as it vanishes and chases the people and situations that play their egotistical games. I will say unto you that there are two forces, one being positive; Love, which comes from the heart and the negative being hatred, which comes from the ego, and becomes control and fear. These two forces are opposites and cannot co-exist. One will eat up and dissolve the other and I say unto you, *"You hold the balance of power!"*

Do you give your power to love or to fear? Are you afraid to Love in case you may get hurt?

As a reader and since I have become aware of this phenomenon, I have observed that if you are afraid to Love, you have lost the battle. You are in fear.

Whatever situation or person faces you, love maybe a lesson, an object or a person, watch as that person or situation transforms into harmony and peace. If you are suffering from a negative experience, it may be the loss of a beloved person or object, understand this is here to teach us a greater lesson, to move us into experiencing a greater love. Love what is gone or what is not or the situation as it is. When it seems like everyone is against you, love them, but first of all, love yourself. When someone you love leaves, they are giving you space to love yourself more and take your power to a heightened plateau and you can immerse yourself in the power of love totally. You can then become the most powerful person on earth. Watch as you continue to love, seeing the people who can't Love be removed from your life, and be replaced with people who can love you as you Love.

The universe is your creation; it mirrors back to you every aspect of yourself. Love yourself, nurture yourself and watch your cup overflow and flow onto others and watch the magical energy flow onto everyone and everything and watch as it transforms the negative into positive. These two forces are opposites and cannot co-exist. One will eat up and dissolve the other and I say unto you, *"You hold the balance of power!"*

The universe is your creation; it mirrors back to you every aspect of your being. Thank the people and the situations as they arise to give you the opportunity to love yourself and others totally and unconditionally. Don't be afraid to Love, because those who cannot love will move away and be replaced by those who can. This repeatedly happens at every turn until you look around you and you are faced with loving people and situations and this is how a Buddha field is created and it has the power to spread like a virus across the globe and heal the world. Be the one, step into your power of true and total Love, become the Buddha or the Christ and Love. Love your friends and their defects, Love your enemies and watch the negative forces retract and dissolve.

Love, my friends, Love—Reap your rewards—Claim your power—Take your place—**LOVE**.

Inspiring Verse
Peace and Joy—Power (flame)

The heart centre—is so important. No matter what the situation, if you go into the heart of the problem, you can fix it—if you don't you only Band-Aid it up. To know the essence you need to go to the heart. It is through the heart that we may know who we are. We may know God and the all that is.

It is through the heart that we can feel and know. Everything else is just a part thereof.

At the heart is the very centre, the very centre of creation. Know thy heart and all is revealed. Know peace and understanding and know every aspect of the all. Know God.

A Message from Archangel Michael and The Rose

We are instruments, helping to guide people who wish to be guided to a lighter vibration. We are overseers, we are protectors and those who ask for our help, receive it, non-judgementally. Anyone who asks for our assistance, receives it in the form of guidance, help or protection. If people choose to listen to the vibration that comes through, they are on their journey to Enlightenment, to the New Earth, to the new world, to a better place. Through the vibration of this book, we aim to give people guidance, to make people interested, to open the door of the mind which in many cases seems to be closed at this time in many on your planet. This can be used as a door of hope, a door of sanity, of light and peace, a feeling of upliftment.

The people on Planet Earth are tired at this time. We feel this. We, the Angels, the guides, the masters and the Saints, give energy to those who desperately need it. To our amazement, they don't change what they do. They continue repeating the same life patterns, which got them into the rut or problem they found themselves in. We then call on various channels which are chosen to help and assist and give messages and healing. The channels are known as Light Workers, which are familiar with the vibration that they are in, and they are asked to help people become aware of what they are involved in and what they are doing or not doing, whatever is the case, and try and get through to them, to get them to listen, to stop, to get them where they can change. To do things differently and this is the aim of the book, to uplift them and help them to lighten their life and their vibration.

Through communicating with the channels and the Light Workers we discovered that all blockages and problems are based on fear, and since then I've been told that there are only two emotions. There is love and there is fear. How the Human Psyche reacts, and it either comes from the Love or Fear. Fear can be, I'm afraid that someone may be going to hurt or harm me, or someone is going to take something from me, or Fear can be, I am going to miss out, and I am not going to have what others have, or I may miss out on opportunities, or I am not going to be as good as others or anything like these. There are all kinds of fear, and may be in many different forms, but fear is a negative, and the absence of Love. Love is positive, and where there is love, there can be no fear. The love I am speaking of, is not romantic in nature, love is something that you feel when you feel good about things, what you are doing, it is creative and makes you feel good, safe, happy and alive, full of energy.

I then asked the Rose (I refer to my spirit friend, the Lady of the Golden Rose. See also section *About the Author* and the end of this book.), *"If you understand that everything is either fear or love, and why am I supposed to channel the Rose"*. Arch Angel Michael replied, *"The Rose, came from a life, which dealt with many egos and emotions of fear and love. The Rose is coming from her understanding of life."* And they started to explain to me that there is one Soul that lives many lives, and has many experiences, and as the soul matures and has dealt with many different scenarios, it gains wisdom, which is even greater than someone who has only lived one life.

And then I replied, *"Please explain to me how to love, how can people love when they are discouraged, disappointed, confused, betrayed, broken? How do you Love and not be afraid that you are going to be hurt when you have gone through so many situations. How do you Trust, how do you Love again?"*

And they said, *"Have you not learned that in the centre core of you, there is light, there is Love, there is God. And God comes through the God Source, of Oneness."* When you meet a person you can unconditionally love, the love in them, the Oneness, the Godliness in them, you can unconditionally love that person, and so God is Loving God. And so it is that God is Loving God, another God, or part of the same god, I should say. In that situation there is no expectation, there is nothing to receive, there is nothing to be taken, there is only loving and sharing.

When you unconditionally love you are giving, the source of the energy comes from the Godliness that you are, the Light that you are, which is the source of all Intelligence, which is all energy. You can never run out of loving or Love because, that is all there is. When you fear, you block the flow of Love, and you try to keep it for yourself, so you block yourself, which is different to loving yourself which is flow. In any shape or form, in anything that you want to do, you either love it or you block it with fear. All fear is and all blockages are the blockage of the energy of source, which is moving through life, which is creativity, which is Life, which is love, which is breath, which is energy, which is water and everything that is.

When you love and you meet a new person or being or animal or whatever, will you curse them or will you love the light that it is in them, the light that is, as it is in you. You do not have to love the mannerisms or personality, the expectations, the desires, the wants, the needs. You only have to love the love, the light in that being and you have no expectations, just love the light, just love the god in that being. This is what we call unconditional love. Because when you have expectations, wants and desires, you are going to create situations to be worked out and you can learn from. People have come to Earth to learn Love, unconditional love. So until they learn that Love, that special kind of love, where there is no fear, where there are no expectations, where they are free to themselves and allow the other to be their true self, then they are going to have situations to show them what love is not. For example, if you don't have a car, and you want a car and to be able take trips and go places, and you meet someone with a nice car, you may begin to love their car and pretend to love them, so they will take you for drives in their car and may even let you drive their car. However, you love the car, not them and eventually situations will arise, because you may not really like them or they may believe you love them and they may think, well, you have a house, so, they will want to share your house and for certain, a situation will arise and you will need to learn that loving their car is not loving them . . . and is not unconditional love.

You are Spirit, Divine in nature, and as a Divine spark of light you only know Love, you only come into the Human Dimension to find what Love is not. Fear is in the material, fear is the desire, the want, the need, the expectation, the thing, which is Fear. Fear is the one thing people have, when they don't feel Love.

Love is flowing light, uncontrolled and just is.

Peace

eace comes from a balanced mind and from balanced emotions. Not from getting what you want. Sometimes obtaining the object or outcome you desire brings more problems and heartache than joy. After many years of struggling, both internally and also dealing with difficult issues and people, I discovered that the only way left or out of a situation was to surrender. Surrender totally unto spirit, my higher self and God. To listen to what God wanted for me, not to that which I wanted, my desires, and my egotistical mind always wanting something. The funny thing is that when I look back, everything that I wanted, I was given, sometimes quicker than I could even realize or understand. What I wanted and was receiving may not have been what I, my mind, my ego, my desire to control wanted. Honestly everything that happened was something I thought of and created first.

It has taken me many years to understand that if we want something, God and the Angels will do everything possible to give it to us, but have no power over another persons' will or their actions or how they will react, for that person, and everyone is a co-creator and has as much power and right to create their world as we do.

God and the Angels can give us the opportunity to play out our desires and it is up to us to work out our Karma and our lessons with the people involved. It seems to me that whilst we are on Planet Earth, we will desire something. For instance, very simply, if we sit still and nothing is happening, eventually a thought or a desire will fleet through our very busy minds. No matter how disciplined spiritually we become, maybe after hours, days, weeks, maybe minutes or even seconds the desire for water will be there. And you may say, *"God, please send me some water."* Be careful, a dam could burst, a flood could wash you away, someone could turn the hose on you, but guaranteed, water, in some form or another will come to you.

We can be more specific, we can ask that someone could bring us a glass of clean fresh cool water. A person we have had problems with in the past or past life could then bring us a glass of clear fresh cool water and decide for some reason to throw the water all over us or just simply trip and spill the water all over us.

The possibilities are endless. God is not a maniac with a wicked sense of humour out to torment and belittle us as much as I have sometimes wondered in the past. God loves us more than we have the capacity to Love. He knows us better than we may even know ourselves and he knows why we are here and what our soul yearns to learn. God knows what it will take to please us, eventually one day we too can understand the parallels between creation, co-creation, existence and co-existence.

We are not alone in this journey of life-. We have people to keep us company and not suffer from loneliness. At times it seems that we are alone. This is the time when we need to look at ourselves, our desires, our selfishness, our control issues, a time to help us to appreciate others and their company. A time to teach us to tolerate other peoples behaviours, even though their actions annoy and disrupt us.

Remember in the beginning there was God and he made man—let's call him Adam. And Adam lived in a Garden, let's name it Earth, and he had everything he wanted and needed and he had control over everything. He or man was kind of a king I suppose. And then one day he was lonely and he said to God, *"I am lonely. If only I had a companion, I could love her, I could share my kingdom with her, I could play and laugh with her and when things go wrong, I could cry with her. We could have an adventure together, see things, and go places together and Love each other."*

And so God created woman and let us call her Eve. So Adam went out of his way to give to Eve and please her as we do when we meet someone new that we like. As Eve would think of something she would like, Adam would try to please her. So this is when the mind kicks in and builds our ego. Now, if I was Eve and this adoring man will give to me anything I desire, my desires could become selfish. And if you have ever watched anyone having this particular lesson unfold, we as humans may see it as people having a good luck stretch in their lives.

The person may win lotto, or a house, or their businesses may boom and fairly soon everything they wish for and more falls before them. And then greed and selfishness and their ego is very well established. Then they begin to forget the basics of love, loyalty, integrity and honesty. Their minds and egos are busy, I'll get a new car, and I'll have two new cars, a rolls and a bigger house. Then I'll have more houses and make more money and desire brings desire. Eventually, I can have a better-looking partner, younger, and have lots of parties and lots of friends and then I can have 2 or 3 or many partners and the list goes on. And we have really gone into self-destruct mode.

We make bigger and bigger wishes and succeed until we destroy ourselves. And then we blame someone else. Our partner, the economy, the government, God, competition, always and always someone or something else is at fault. Can you see our minds go on creating what is really an illusion, for it is based on ego? And the ego is not truth and only truth sustains. Many an empire, even civilizations, many a marriage, partnership have fallen and when they reach rock bottom, they scream out, *"God help me! Is there a God? God, why me? Why?"*

When our own egotistical traits have lead us to our own downfall and we let ourselves down, then we call out for help. Then we begin to soul search and really the whole process is very beautiful, because we have led ourselves into temptation. And our egos, our minds, our selfishness get out of hand and we lose ourselves and then we search to find our true self and begin again with a new understanding. Then this process is repeated until only the truth stares back at us. Then we appreciate ourselves and begin to build on a new foundation, and what we then create can be so beautiful. Once we have learned to love ourselves, then we will love God and everyone and everything else. We then create beauty and love and only then does our world know and understand peace. You will become at peace and in harmony with the flow of life, in all its many paradigms.

Giving
Channeled by the Lady of the Golden Rose

Blessings, to each and to all of you, my message and the insight that we give is about giving. Many people have spoken and speak all around the world talking about Love. Loving unconditionally and loving and being and giving. Few people understand the concept we speak of in Giving Love freely.

Anything that is to happen is energy. It can be transformed into manifestation into physical or it can stay in the Ethereal or in the Mental Body as ideas and inspiration but it is all energy. Everything is energy. Even the chair that we sit on is energy, concentrated energy, which has come into a form. When the chair has had its day, and the energy wants to move on, it will fall apart and is then dispersed into the atmosphere to be recycled once again. A thought comes, it is energy. A thought can come, you can think it, you can understand the thought, you can let it go and it can disperse, or you can hold onto the thought, and manifest it into a form. Love is the energy. Love can come, love can pass through, or you can hold onto it, and you may deepen your love, and transfer that love that you are feeling onto people, or things, or animals, or pets or gardens, or even roses, or anything that you want. But, if you hold onto that love, or that energy, it must form into something. For example, when you feel the energy of love, a person may come into your life to take shape and form. It maybe a lover, for some it could be the birth of a child, or maybe an adoption, or grandchildren, for some it may be taking in a border, for some it could be partners, of loving relationships or marriage, or someone or thing that you have wanted. But all these people are forms of the love you felt coming through you from Divine Source.

So this loving, this living is all energy in movement, in motion. When you hold onto it, it takes form, but form is not permanent. Form cannot be forever. So it must be formed, and be there and then disperses. Even the mountains and the oceans move on and change, through the help of earth quakes, volcanoes and war. Things change. This is the nature of the whole Universe, is to be moving on. When the form of your life, comes to its expiry date, it will transform into a new life. The Lord Jesus, Jeshua, The Christ, went on the cross to show people how his form would transform into a new life. Not be dead and buried, but be transformed into new living, new consciousness, in a new realm. So the only way that things move on is through form, is through giving. You are given energy to breath, to think, to do, to garden, to meet with others, to love others-. This energy comes from Source. Source created everything, everything, at all times is Source. There are different time frames, time realities, time illusions, they are all through movement of energy coming into form and then dispersing. So if you want to be clear, the more you give, in whatever way is yours to give, it keeps yourself moving, with reality, with Christ, with Consciousness, with God.

The more you have, whatever you have, we say to you give. Give because the Universe gave it to you, and if you don't use it and share it, you are going to lose it. This is my message today. If you don't live your life, people, they get old, they get weary, and they forget to live, so they are moved onto a new existence where they'll be fresh again. If you are stale and stagnant in your job, you will lose it and you will find a new job, and start afresh and hopefully be more enthusiastic, if you are not, you will lose that job. If you have a car, and you don't look after your car or you don't like it, you will lose it in some shape or form and you will get another one and if you don't love this one, and look after it and use it, you will lose that one too.

So every obstacle, every stoppage in your life is something within you, not allowing you to let it flow. This is why we say to you, if you have anger, or negative emotions, let them be out there, get rid of them, let them flow on so that you do not hold onto them and dam up your energy of flow.

Your Heart centre, your Solar Plexus, are all energy points for energy to flow through, if they stop flowing then you stop in your tracks and this is where disaster can happen. Keep moving, keep moving on, keep giving, we are not saying to abandon your money and give it to someone else. That is not what we are saying at all. We are saying when you have time to help somebody, help them, when you have time to teach somebody, teach them, if for some reason, that a beggar approaches you, you don't have to give them everything, but if you give a small amount that helps, the energy can flow, is the way to go. We also want to remind you that you can never lose anything that is yours. If you were cheated out of your money or belongings, or you lose something that is of value to you, and you haven't let it go in the ethereal, than whatever is yours, will be returned to you in some shape or form. If this thing that you believe is lost and disappears, just say to your Angels, *"If it is mine, it shall be returned"*. But if you lose something, for example, your car is in an accident and nobody was hurt, ask yourself, *"Did I really love that car, did I really want that particular car?"* if you did than you would have loved it so much that you would have insured it and it will be returned in another shape or form, but maybe you didn't love it so much and you will appreciate the new one even more than the one before.

Even if you release and give something very small, it will begin the process, a little bit, by little bit, begins to unblock things. Then the more you give, the more you will be appreciated, and any appreciation is quite a high vibration. We also acknowledge that the art of appreciation may seem quite scarce at this time in society. Have you ever been appreciated? To be appreciated feels so uplifting, feels so good, as if you have accomplished something wonderful, especially if someone actually goes out of their way, to give a small gift of appreciation, or some small gesture, even to take the time to say, "thank you, you have helped me". It unblocks some of the blockages and you want to flow on and to give some more. But when you are giving you are helping somebody, you are lightening up their world, and then the appreciation comes, for you to unblock some more of your stuff and you can give more, more and more.

But it is not taking from you, and giving to someone else, it is sharing what you have. So that you are more, the more that you are sharing, the more energy you allow to flow through you which will indeed allow more to come to you. It is only when you are holding back that the blockages occur and you will get less energy.

If you hold onto anything and it dams up and becomes a negative emotion, if this happens to a person, what is the easiest way to release that? You need to look within yourself. The quickest and easiest way, is to give it away or let it go. But if that is the problem, we then ask you to go within and find out why you are holding onto this negative emotion and to work with it until you can let it go. We know that in the course of your interactions with others it can be easy to hold onto many emotions, and through meditation and our instructions, it is coming to the understanding of the gift of giving and loving.

It has been said that all blockages are based on fear, and since then I've been told that there are only two basic emotions. There is love and there is fear. People react, either from Love or Fear. Fear can be, I'm afraid that someone may be going to hurt or harm me, or someone is going to take something from me, or Fear can be, I am going to miss out, and I am not going to have what others have, or I may miss out on opportunities, or I am not going to be as good as others or anything like these. There are all kinds of fear, and may be in many different forms, but fear is negative, the absence of Love. And Love is positive, and where there is Love, there can be no fear.

There is one Soul that lives many lives, and people often feel that they are going to be hurt when they have gone through so many situations, and often ask, *"How do you Trust, How do you Love again?"* And it is said, *"Have you not learned that in the centre core of you, there is light, is Love, is God".* And God comes through the God Source, of Oneness. When you meet a person you can unconditionally love, the love is in them. The Oneness, the Godliness is in them and you can unconditionally love that person, and so the God part of you is loving the God part of them, and so God is loving God. There is no expectation, there is nothing to receive, there is only loving and giving.

So when you are unconditionally loving you are giving, the source of the energy comes from the Godliness that you are, the Light that you are, which is the source of all Intelligence, all energy. You can never run out of loving or Love because, that is all there is. When you fear, you block the flow of Love, and you try to keep it for yourself, so you block yourself, which is different to loving yourself which is flow. In any shape or form, in anything that you want to do, you either love it or you block it with fear. All fear is and all blockages are the blockage of the energy of source, moving through you, which is creativity, which is Life, which is love, which is breath, which is energy and everything that is.

However some people are quite fixed in holding onto habits or obsessions or things like this, and we do appreciate that these blockages may have been brought about by painful and disappointing experiences, but we have a practise that may help you with your release of your blockages and burdens. Yes, if you can identify the source of why you have developed the blockage or the disease the discomfort, then by releasing that, you can heal.

Practise to Release Blockages

We invite you to join with us in a simple but effective practise. Now take a deep breath into a light meditative state. Can each and every one of you discern a blockage, of some description? This may be an emotion, a habit, a feeling, a pain, an illness, something that is not going ahead in your life or maybe even be a fear. We want you to focus on that blockage. Become aware of what emotions this blockage is bringing to the surface, and we understand that we are all dealing with different kinds of blockages. That is perfectly fine. Just focus on the blockage, and understand that there will be a sharp emotion underneath and it will rise, it could be one of fear, it could be one of all kinds of things, whatever it is, have we all got that sharp emotion?

Now we want to ask, *"Where does that emotion come from?"*

From what cause, from what stage, and some of you may have to use your intuition, as this may go back longer than you can remember consciously.

Take a deep breath, and your guides will help you if that is needed or required. Where did this emotion come from?

Do you have your answers now?

Okay, you have your answer. So now, we want you to formulate some sort of shape or symbol, in front of you, see a shape or symbol that symbolises to you, your fear or emotion that you are dealing with. Can you do that? Do you have your symbol?

Now we want you to allow it to release and take a large breath and blow it out with your out-going breath, see it going to the light. Blow!

And begin, see it, and blow it out. And as you blow it, you will see it begin to dissolve, and go into the Ethers, into the light and dissolve.

Once again, see your symbol, whatever your symbol looks like, is fine. And on the count of three, imagine a beautiful light, where you'll blow your symbol too, as it dissolves, evaporates you feel your discomfort, your illness, your fear whatever you began with, you feel it leave and you become lighter and clear of your blockage, if the blockage was being blocked, you will find the inspiration, the answer, even the answers to whatever was holding you back.

Put your hands on the top of your legs, palms upwards, and give thanks to the Universe, Your God, Your creator, that your fears, your illness, your blockages, your habits whatever, is now gone. And as you have given, then you will receive the faith to know that it is all going to be transformed. NOW!

And so it is . . . Do you feel lighter?

You are Spirit, Divine in nature, and as a Divine spark of light you only know Love, you only come into the Human Dimension to find what Love is not. Fear is only found in the material, the third dimension, fear is the desire, is the want, the need, the expectation, the thing, the blockage that is Fear.

Love is flowing light, energy, uncontrolled by the mind or ego and just is.

This practise may be repeated every day until you see a change.

Continuation of Giving—the Rose

I wish to continue with the earlier chapter in this book called Giving.

People give gifts on your planet, in your time space, they give to each other, they buy things, and it is like a symbol of their love, their appreciation, and in some cases their regards to that person. We want to talk about giving gifts from the heart. In order to give from the heart, the heart needs to open. You cannot give a gift from the heart if the heart is closed. But the heart is a very sensitive organ, (chakra), the heart centre is also a very sensitive energy point, both can be hurt extremely easily.

It takes a strong heart to dissipate the energy that is shafted towards it on occasions, and to keep going, and to keep on loving, and to keep on giving. But if you could understand that the Heart is an energy centre, and the material heart is a pumping station. It feeds out and it feeds in. The Heart can feed in all the things that are going on in your outside world, and if you imagine your heart centre as a windmill and as it goes round, the heart pumps, the real heart pumps the blood in from the rest of your organs. It filters the blood and then it sends out fresh blood, loving, fresh and clean blood to feed your organs again. In the heart energy centre, you are taking in the energy perhaps of the outside world and your experiences and sending it around and sending out what you have received from that experience. We would ask, or suggest, that you could possibly look at a new source, of the energy flow, that new source could be the Golden Light. For if you can reach the Golden Light in meditation, and can feel the essence of love emanating from that energy, source energy, from that being or perhaps realm, and you were feeding that through your windmill, or through your heart, through your energy centre, you can then imagine this being a much more beneficial gift to receive.

Instead of taking in the outer circumstances, the situations that you believe you are receiving from other people, and you changed your inlet from the outside world to the higher realms of Godliness, the Golden Spirit, of the realm of love, and fed that through your energy centre, and fed that into the world instead of recycling old gifts of love, you would be bringing something new and more loving into being. This is the energy we wish you to be bringing in.

With meditation, you can reach those higher realms and higher vibrations. It is good if you can stay connected to those higher realms. We are not saying that some people don't on this earth. We want to assist more people to experience this energy and have more people sharing this energy. It is like, if someone gives you a gift, perhaps it may be a statue, and you give this statue to somebody else, to somebody else and somebody else, it will get old. It is stale, and down the line people will notice it is scratched and or dented, and it has lost its newness, whereas, if you give them a new gift, a new energy, it is always appreciated more than something that is passed on. So we are saying that instead of rehashing the love that you are running around with, we want you to bring in the new love, the new energy vibration, (a slightly lighter vibration). It is like instead of the old blood going round and round in your body, and the heart pumping and pumping it and pumping it, we want to give you a transfusion, and the new blood that will be going around and around and around will have tiny cellulites of gold in it, sparkling gold of a higher vibration, of a lighter vibration. With the new energy comes more benefits which will help people to connect and love each other more easily with less criticism, more caring.

How do people raise their vibration to the energy of the heart centre to feel this new vibration?

The answer is by finding a space in your world, or in your mind through meditation, which enables you to feel the higher love vibration. Perhaps by being in nature more and meditating more, by praying more. There is a new energy, which you can tap into, a new energy source, a higher vibration available to your plane of existence now, available to your higher consciousness now.

I would like to take you on a guided meditation: A guided visual exercise to share—

Guided Visualisation

If you would like to close your eyes, and just breathing in the energy that is here today, and imagine you are walking outside, leave the house behind, the sky is a beautiful indigo colour, magical and mystical. And when you walk outside you may notice a nice cool breeze, feel the freshness in the air, you can almost hear the trees breathing, breathing in and breathing out, there is so much light and energy in the air, and moisture. It is a sparkling night, a glistening night. You look up and see the glistening, sparkling stars, perhaps the moon, and I want you to find a star, a huge glistening shiny star, or perhaps you can use the moon, whichever you think is more appropriate, but I would prefer you to use a star, for a star is another sun, and it has a lot more energy, because it gives energy, and we want you to find that sparkling, shiny glistening star and we want you to look at it, see that star coming closer or you moving closer to it, see it becoming larger and larger, and larger, and as you breath in I want you to connect with that star and see a stream of light, connecting you with that star. That star is actually a sun from another universe, which is giving you energy. Visualize your heart and your mind being connected to this star. As you are being filled up with this golden energy. And you go closer and closer until this star is so huge, that all you see is the shining golden light of the star, you see it pulsating, sending energy to you. This transformative energy is the new energy that is available. And it is filling your veins, your mind, your heart, and your solar plexus, right down to the tips of your toes. It is a beautiful strong energy, and you should almost feel your body changing, pulsating, tingling, changing, vibrating, and you may not be able to describe this energy, but it feels good, and you will want some more of it. So more of it comes, and fills you, until you are overflowing with this energy. And you point to your loved ones and your friends that are coming towards you. You see this energy streaming forth into their hearts, and around them, you see them filling up with this golden light. For this energy is so powerful, it may equate to love or it may equate to something else, it might equate to ice cream if you love ice cream, but know that it is just very good for you and you will want more of it, and more of it, and more of it. It feels so good you will want to share it with others, because you haven't felt this good for a long time and neither have they. Everyone seems to have felt tired and empty, they have felt dull and flat for some time now. As you share this energy with your friends and loved ones, you will feel that you are getting charged with the energy right now, and you can't take anymore in so you have to point to your friends and your loved ones and fill them up with it as well. And as you give it to them, you feel even more energised. You can see this energy being pumped all through your being, all through your mind, your third eye, all the chakras, all your body, all your body parts, all the connections in your body being charged with this super energy and loving it, and you don't know what it is, but it feels so good . . . . and this energy not only has the power to make you feel good, it has the power to make you clean, it has the power to make your mind clear, it has the power to make you well, it has the power to transform you right now. Right now we ask you, to see a symbol of what it is that you would like to change in your life, it can be health, it may be your career, it can be anything you want. If you are feeling the energy, if you believe in this new energy, it will heal what you want it to heal, right now. And the healing process will begin.

And so it is and it is done.

Time To Wake Up

Have you taken a moment out of your busy day recently, given thought about your world recently? We are indeed experiencing strange weather patterns and threatening signs of violent storms, tornadoes, fires, earth-quakes and volcanoes and even pending war. For those of you who are aware, take heed, the signs are here and prepare yourself for the rapid changes our world is about to undergo, both on a personal level and also on a holistic level.

For many, yes! These are indeed the signs we have been anticipating. So let go of your attachments to the way things should be in your view, go and take advantage of the ever present opportunities being presented before you now. Many of us have known that we were put on this Earth at this time, to fulfil a profound and meaningful purpose. Many of you know the purpose, others know something, but not sure of the details. Rejoice and know that what you do know is enough to lead you safely to fulfilling your purpose and through the mass ignorance and indifference and in some cases, actual contempt and negative perceptions, judgements and even surroundings. Your awareness will indeed guide you to your soul's purpose, enabling you to fulfil your role with skilful and tactful assurance that something is happening on a deep and profound level of awakening.

For those who are unaware of this awakening, this chapter is to reassure you that great change is imminent and ask you to consider your world, your motivations, where you are at and what does it all mean to you? Are you at peace and content with what you have created all around you and within? Are you complete and whole and ready to advance to a new stage of development without getting caught up in all the hype (hypocrisy), the ignorance and the arrogance of the unsuspecting which will lead to complete and utter chaos both within and without? And one day could lead to hardship and catastrophic devastation.

I suggest while you still have time between your robotic like programmed careers, and busy social lives, you stop and take a moment to reflect on where you are at. Living in fictitious worlds of distractions, which dissolve into oblivion and you, convince yourself that your reality has no real meaning in consciousness. Indeed, it is time to take a second and reflect on our world, our life. Time seems to have sped up. Sometimes the day is at its' close when we feel like we just woke up and got started. Our life has become almost frantic trying to fit all the tasks and appointments in to our daily schedule, and so routine that we can almost do it with our eyes closed or unconsciously. Have we forgotten that there is a beautiful world to enjoy? One which has roses to smell, beautiful scenery to enjoy, great oceans and seashores to reflect upon and heal from, fresh air to breathe in and birds that sing and seemingly talk to you if only you had time to connect and be with them and enjoy. Take some time to walk in the rain, ponder on the beautiful rainbow and talk to your angels, your guides or even yourself.

For most of us, we have got all caught up, trying to keep up with the rent or the mortgage, the newest computer or telephone that can do everything for you except think for you, or the largest television screen and the loudest sound system that we forgot who we really are and what we are really all about, except trying to hold onto that unobtainable dollar.

When you sit on the train or bus and glance at the people around you. You meet stone like gazes with no apparent signs of life or personality. Gripping ever so tightly to their grim, no interest facades, almost afraid to drop their cool exterior in case someone takes a moment of their fragile existences and shows them a smile or dares to say, *"Good Morning"*. And if they did, would you die of shock or would you ignore them, and move on, afraid to open to another soul, a beautiful human being who may share some trinket of information that could enlighten or help you. The risk may be too great, it may be you who lends a hand or helps in some way, or you who needs the help or the insight.

No, we need a few scotches under our belts before we can loosen our grip or let down our guard and relax for a few short moments. Often, that comes only when our consciousness is taken to a drunken state and we can really let go of our pent up feelings and dribble a lot of nonsense for no apparent reason, which often ends up offending others rather than closing the gap of separateness. Let me say folks, it's time to drop our facades and to discover that under each of our many disguises, there is a beautiful soul, just waiting for the opportunity to express itself in truth, an eternal Soul seeking love, acceptance and appreciation. Wake up now, before there is no more time, no more opportunities to awaken.

Know Thyself First

When we think about who we are, in the present moment, where we are going and what we want and want to achieve, we may find that we are all caught up in our heads, in wishes, hopes, dreams and desires. Do we see ourselves in reality, or through others expectations and desires? Do we see our future and our goals in false expectations? Could this be the reason some of us continually fall down after trying and trying and working hard to convince everybody and ourselves that we should be successful in some line or another and it doesn't work the way we wish it to? Could it possibly be because we have only seen our false hopes, wishes and desires and not our true identity and skills and talent? Do we sometimes set goals and have ambitions beyond our capability and ability to achieve and maintain? Then we are burdened with the pressure of keeping up our charades and high ideals and push ourselves further beyond our limits in an attempt to outdo what we've done till now. The pressure and burdens create raised tempers, irritable personalities, high blood pressure, headaches, breakdowns and eventually depressed states of being. Ultimately we get to feel very sorry for ourselves, how we are overworked and underpaid; nobody cares and the "poor me," syndrome. We continue to feel sorry for ourselves, until somebody or another situation appears and feels sorry for us, picks us up and helps us to recover and then we continue around the merry-go-round once again, trying to be someone we were never intended to be. Someone with greatness, success, always doing and doing, more and more; hoping to achieve greatness in someone else's eyes. Then when greatness happens, quite often we have exhausted ourselves, trying so hard to impress others, but can we maintain this pressure, and for how long? Until the bubble bursts once again, and then we fall into a heap and cry out for help again.

Hence, the pattern continues over and over again until we find a plateau and begin building ourselves up again to the next level of greatness, needing to do better than our previous display of success and reach greater heights than before, always trying to perfect something, someone or ourselves. The next best seller, larger pay packets, longer trips more expensive homes and cars, bigger and better and on we go.

When does lasting happiness, and success come? When and how do we find peace? When have we overcome the last challenge, set back and disaster? When are we running smoothly, and achieving success without stress and pressure? When are we content with what we have achieved and who we are? When do desires and dreams give way to fulfilment and enjoyment?

Meditation showed me that rainbows are made of hopes, dreams, and wishes, which are beautiful, however are only temporary. The proverbial pot of gold at the end of the rainbow may not be wealth and riches in the material sense anyway, but maybe the realization of truth, sincerity and honour. It maybe that we need to acknowledge who we are, not our desires and aspirations of who we may become, the greatness of who we already are. Seeing in truth that we are good enough just doing and being ourselves. Being honest with ourselves, and acknowledging who we are as a person, friend, parent, child, and seeing ourselves, physically, emotionally and spiritually, worthwhile just being ourselves. We need to know who we really are, be comfortable with who we are and what we can do and do well without over doing anything that causes stress or pain. Can we accept who we really are and honour that person, that soul, without expectation or desire and without aspiring to be someone other than ourselves? Our wishes, dreams, aspirations and expectations, usually lead to disappointments, unfulfilled dreams and desires and burst bubbles and wasted time, instead of mastering all that we already are.

Just think if everybody mastered who they were and trusted and honoured God and the great plan because everyone has their own unique beauty and talent, which is their gift to this reality. We could begin to build and be a part of that beautiful grand picture that was intended instead of fighting, being envious or jealous and in conflict with others as well as with ourselves. We could paint and be a part of that picture of perfection, love, serenity and peace.

Perfect that which you are and you will automatically become all that you can be with ease and grace, instead of chasing false hopes and dreams that last as long as a rainbow.

Most of us don't even know ourselves, who and what we are, and what we are really capable of, never mind mastering anything, and yet as we master the basics of who we are, the rest will just automatically fall into place, if only we can trust the universe and allow the beauty to unfold spontaneously. If we are tired and worn out trying to be someone or something, take a deep breath of fresh air, and look a little deeper at who you are right now. And so it has been written *"Know thyself and then all things shall come to light"*.

When you are indeed comfortable with who you are, knowing your strength and your weaknesses and placing the correct boundaries, you are then ready to follow your passion, your true hearts' desire, and become all that your creator had planned for you when you came into this world, with ease and grace, knowing you are fulfilling your perfect purpose.

Aloneness—The Greatest Friend and Teacher

The struggle of relationships; the battles we fight to maintain a partner, a friend, or even a confidante. We endure many seeming abuses, insults and feelings of hurt and pain, just so we don't have to live with that person we see when we look in the mirror. We endure pitiful relationships that show little respect for ourselves by way of—, support, nurturing or love. Why???? To avoid being alone, avoid living solely with self, maybe even avoiding knowing who that self really is and certainly to avoid an intimate and loving relationship with oneself. How many people bend and twist themselves to make someone else the king or queen of their life and feel only too happy to oblige others requests and eventually find out that they don't have a life of their own. They don't have their own friends or interests and if that other half or three quarters ever decides to desert them, their life seemingly is hollow and empty. How many people are emotionally crippled and feel they can't go on, when that other person or pet leaves or even dies. Most people become crippled. They search and search for another partner or pet, still failing to find the greatest possible friend they could ever have; themselves.

And yet, for the people who do for whatever reason spend time to get to know, like and love themselves, become whole beings and enjoy their solace, they usually make the best relationships. If people are willing to share their sanctuary, they will create the healthiest relationships because they are not co-dependent on someone else to make them happy. Yes I believe that you will see God in every person you meet, but if you don't know God first hand, how will you ever recognize God in anyone else?

73

How many of us get up in the morning, see ourselves in the mirror, smile and say good morning. More likely we run and hide or don't even look into the mirror for if we have to spend one more day alone with that person, we may scream. FACT; If we don't like who looks back at us in the mirror, why would you even think that someone else would like them?

Does that person in the mirror show you understanding, love you, have compassion and care what your day is going to be like? Do they care what anyone else's day is going to bring? Or is that person only engrossed on what is not going their way, how things could be better and what they have missed out on? Have a good look in the mirror. What does that person look like? What do they do for you and then everyone else? And if that person in the mirror checks off even our greatest criticisms, why aren't we happy and content being solely in our own company, and in fact being a little more protective, and choose our friends a little more discerningly. It all comes back to each individual we meet is showing us a part of ourselves. Is that part all loving and caring or do we need to do a little work on ourselves?

Working in this field as long as I have, it still amazes me at the experiences I drawer to myself. What we believe, really does dictate our life and how it works out. If we are aware enough, we can see why we drawer certain experiences to us and then we can change our beliefs so that we don't need to learn that lesson over again. If you seem to be repeating certain facets of your life, or if you are saying, *"that's how it always works out."* Then do something about your beliefs, or how much you love and care for yourself. Change your beliefs!!! What we believe truly is the author of our lives, so take time to get to know, like and love the author of your life. They truly are the most important person you will ever meet. In the morning when you look in the mirror, if you can't see a wonderful, caring and loving person you are pleased to smile and bless, then do the work, change what you don't like and put a lasting smile on your face.

I wish everybody who comes into my shop a happy day on a daily basis and I mean it. Because if I can get through my day still wishing people happiness, joy and love, then, I know that blessing is coming back to me, perhaps even tenfold or more. Love the person who greets you first thing every morning and watch the loving people move into your life. And the best thing is, that if there is only you, you still have a wonderful time with only the best people. God bless you in your aloneness. You may be the best friend you will ever have.

The Truth
Shall Set You Free

In this world that we are moving into, it feels chaotic, impersonal, and basically a survival of the fittest or the most intelligent, or the most deceitful, hungry, or greediest. It feels that people, the majority, I am speaking about are preoccupied with a shortage of Time, and overfull Diary of appointments to keep and an obsession to paying the credit card and keeping up with this fast paced erratic world and their friends and acquaintances. From my observation, people more and more are living on the outer, or the surface of their identity, and know very little about the inner World, their inner being, and the sanctuary that lies within. Where people can live a quiet filled peace, of authenticity and revel in being who they were intended to be, to care and to cherish life, one another and themselves. A place of existence, where they can be one with God, the Universe, their Angels and Guides, where there is kindness and tranquillity and sanctuary of Peace.

How do we find that peace, that centre of our being? When we don't have a moment from one deadline to the next, when our fuel tanks of energy are running near on empty with no reserves?

From my own personal experience of life and also watching many lives unfold in front of me doing clairvoyant and psychic readings, we seem to need to run the rat race, jump the hurdles, push ourselves beyond our limits, avoiding ourselves, our inner most self; until the inevitable happens, and our illusion cracks, and we hit that brick wall. We have an accident, we lose our job, our relationship goes down the drain, we suddenly find we could be looking at going into bankruptcy, friends leave us in swarms, somebody close, whom we may have also neglected, becomes very ill or dies. Then the reality of who we have become, begins to surface and our super hero persona begins to shrivel. Then we begin to search for that true identity, "who am I?"

At some stage of our insane attempts to avoid ourselves, something will bring us back to the need to reassess our lie and begin to dig for a truth that is concrete, that endures the test of time, ageing and weathers the storms and keeps us safe and secure in an ever changing world of deception and illusion.

It seems to me that, every time we consciously make a significant change in our lives, we move house, we change our job, even our career, we change cars, we are searching for that true us to stand up and be known. We are searching for our persona on the outside, in a world that really doesn't care or matter, when all we have to do is breath. Become aware of our breath, focus on our breathing, watch our breathing, and we will find all the answers of who we are in the inside. The person on the inside is the one that is with us and stays the same all of our lives, in fact all of eternity . . . and our whole journey of searching for who we are; years, lives was all for us to wake up and realise that the whole universe is within ourselves, that we are indeed living, breathing beings of Light with infinite potential and possibilities.

We dwell in a false reality and some of us seek the almost impossible, to grasp the Truth, the Real, the Lasting, and when you make that journey to the centre of who you are; you will meet the oneness, the Gift of Life, The Supreme Intelligence, The Master Mind, The Ultimate Consciousness. Then we can build on an eternal foundation. The surface may once again crumble, may not endure the changing and fragmenting cycles of time, but our foundation, our beliefs, our knowing remains intact and we can learn and rebuild and rebuild without the devastation of total loss and Identity crisis. Once we understand the meaning of life, we know our true selves and we discover that everything we do in this life, is a step towards our true selves, everything becomes a joy. We will come to realise that the only constant in this world is change, constructive or destructive, but change is the only way forward.

I have heard people through their logic believe that because God, Ultimate Intelligence, Cosmic Consciousness is within, then this Intelligence or Power can make them great or at least feel as if they are special, or more special than others. My understanding is that as we grow in awareness through meditation, and can tap into one finite Intelligence, the God Mind, that it is greater than what we can possibly comprehend and it is our Ego's who become boosted, for the power and intelligence of all that is, even though it is a living consciousness that we can tap into. This living consciousness is far more intelligent and superior than we could ever hope to gain control of. An analogy could be, that it is as if we are a 16-watt instrument, and can tap into high voltage wires that carry all the electricity to different cities, and if we were to plug directly into that high voltage, we would explode or burst into flames. Do not allow your ego to fry you.

Sometimes, it is better knowing, and accepting that we are a part of the greatest intelligence that ever existed. We are a channel and we channel that intelligence, that energy. We are a part of the whole and indeed that whole is within, but each and every one of us has that same potential that same reality that same eternal flame of creativity and Intelligence as the God Head and All that is.

Self Empowerment

Recently through many situations arising and unexpected events, opportunities, traumas and plans ending in various forms of failure, deceit, relief and success, I have come to understand and to realize what it means to be self-empowered.

This is a new stage of my development, so as it unveils more and more, I will know what it means to realize the potential of the power within my being. For now, my experience makes me aware of how I can channel negative energy into positive. Look at negative outcomes and see them as stepping stones to greater opportunities and become so self-empowered that no-one or situation from the outside has any influence over my being, that is to say my direction, how I choose to feel and see things and my choices.

As I awoke into this realization, I became aware of certain energies placed upon me with the intention of keeping me in a certain frame of mind or influencing my decisions, which allowed other people to see something that may not have been truth. But the greatest part of this realization was becoming aware that some of these energies were placed there because I allowed and even wanted them there, and realizing that no one has any energy or power over me unless I choose to let it be there.

To give you an idea of some of the energies I am speaking of. Have you ever been in a relationship and no matter how hard you try to break free of it or the other person, something keeps bringing you back? Some people believe these situations arise because of the Law of Karma, or the other person is more powerful than we are, hence giving away our power totally or we can choose; do we stay in this 'no win' situation or do we simply empower ourselves and move away, make a new life for ourselves?

I am here to tell you, it is your choice. As a clairvoyant reader, many people have come to me and asked about relationships they are not happy in, saying that they cannot break away from, or something holds them back. The only thing that holds them to any situation is their own choice, which may be hope, faith or desire for something to happen or a fear of moving on independently.

Self-empowerment can only happen in the present moment, when you make a decision and if you choose with awareness in every moment you won't lose your power ever again. If you give a person or a situation or a desire a chance, it can eat up your power totally and you will once again become a victim. Self-empowerment means you are never a victim again. When you make a choice or a decision and it turns out wrong or not the way you believed or hoped it would be, take stock of yourself, own your decision and the outcome. Understand this is an opportunity for something else to take place, for you to learn and grow from.

If you are let down, or disappointed or even angered, accept that this is how you feel, don't give all your energy to it. Confess to yourself that you are feeling disappointed, angry, and even hurt. Look at your part in the event and look at it as an opportunity to take your power and walk on and move into a new adventure or situation. Pain only comes when you won't accept the situation, and when you refuse to let go of the past, when your expectations are not fulfilled, when your desires are not met and fulfilled.

Self-empowerment means when you make the right decisions through consciousness and awareness. When you put the energy into something and you manifest life the way you want it to be. When this does not happen, look through the process and see what part you didn't do one hundred percent, then take responsibility and be daring and honest with yourself. Ask why it didn't work. Accept a truthful answer even if you don't like it and move on.

Life is an adventure and you are living it. It is your choice to enjoy it or not. To hold onto it or let it go. Whatever you choose, choose consciously. Another lesson I learned through my experiences is to set my boundaries. To understand what is acceptable and what is not, being fully aware that nothing is right or wrong, but where do I draw the line for myself? Where is my boundary between like and love, like and dislike, giving and being taken, forgiveness and abuse—acceptable and unacceptable.

Know your boundaries and in doing so, you can know and accept yourself. Your choices become simpler, when someone or a situation moves beyond the boundary, then and in that moment you exercise full control and take your power and move on in life.

Life is for living and exploring and enjoying. Pain equals the past and if you are in pain, let it go, for your pain from the past will colour your present and your future. Thank the situation, the people involved and God for the experience. Learn from it and let it go. Take the positive and let go of anything that is not positive. There are so many other things in life you can experience and enjoy.

Know you gave your best and if you didn't, then know that it is something within you that really didn't want the outcome. And if you gave it your best, then know that it is not for you at this time and something better and greater is about to happen if you are one hundred percent present and aware. Be ready and willing to move into your next experience joyfully and be in your power. Make the choices that you want to see happen. Peace, be with you all.

Freedom

The time is now, not tomorrow, not yesterday, now! The time to change, to improve, to clear or discard is now. Every desire, thought, feeling, emotion, connected to attachment is holding you back from being present and in this moment. To take advantage of being in this moment, one needs to be clear! How can one be clear when their vision is full of emotion from yesteryear, objects that may have been lost, or desires of the future, things and time that has not yet come to pass?

To clear the vision, clear the attachments, one walks forward alone. If you are carrying things, feelings, emotions, memories, people, the walk forward is cluttered and burdened. Even to the point that the burdens may be so heavy, so as to cause you to falter or even fall into the past.

Release all attachments and burdens and walk freely forward. Freedom is being unburdened and unattached. It is purely your choice. Attachments can be emotional, physical, or of the mind. You can continue if you wish, on a long path or journey. Although sometimes it is refreshing to rest awhile and even renew. Remember, if you take something from a place of rest or any sacred sight, or place of worship, or if you gain something, maybe even an insight always be sure to return it to where it belongs or give something else back, even as simple as a thank you. You may think that an appreciation or "thank you" is nothing, but that is so far from the Truth. Saying "thank you" even in your mind is a vibration or energy. This has the intent of appreciation. When you say thank you even in your mind and it is sincere and heart-felt, it is a very high vibration and; something to be cherished. Know how valuable it is to hear someone you have helped, assisted or given something to, say "thank you," and understand, that the vibration is uplifting and very, real. Or you may wish to clear the energy completely or else the path ahead can become so steep, and yesterdays' burden can become so heavy that they can slow you down, hold you up or even pull you right back to where they belong; in the past.

BE FREE! The path of Freedom is easy, not complicated, not restricted in any manner. It is for clear sailing, and Clarity is of the utmost importance. It is for moving into a new world or realm, making decisions and building a new foundation, which can only happen in the now.

Being free means that you are free to be yourself at all times. You live with integrity, you are clear in your opinions, you live in your truth. You set your heart, notice I said heart and not mind to what you feel is right for you at this time and you move forward without fear. Being free means there is no fear, no restrictions and no barriers. You are then free to live out your truth in all of its entirety, respecting the law of Karma. What you put out, you will experience and understand that you are your creator, you are your judge and your jury. Be free my friends, and live. Move forward and live the life you desire, by paying all debts, forgiving all processes of the past, and being happy with your consciousness and who you are.

Oneness

At the core of each union is 'oneness'. For if you are not one at the root or the beginning—there will always be a split. True union can only happen or sustain when there is a oneness at the root, at the beginning. If the root is one—the two can flower and spread in all directions, but will always return to the root and each time this is revisited, then it can become stronger and merge and twine into eternal light together growing stronger and more powerful until there is only one.

The one will always return home when it has fulfilled its need to be separate. Separate entities cannot co-exist for long for at the root they are different. And we must always return to the root for sustenance. Allow the spirit to weave its magick and allow the union to unfold in its own glorious light and fragrance for others to experience this essence of oneness.

I am the Light, the power and the universe. I am not God, for God brings in a feeling of something without each of us and I am the light beyond comprehension. I am that which no mind can ever hope to understand or analyse or discern. I am neither good nor bad, light nor dark, for where there is light there is no darkness, there is no duality.

Where I am and who or what I am, there is no illusion, there is nothing and yet everything. There is only dark and light when you are outside of one or the other. When you stand submerged in light, no darkness is possible. When in darkness, no light is possible until you step back out of the dark.

When in this energy of light—pure light, miracles do not happen—nothing happens. The miracles happen when you bring this light into darkness. When you are the source of power, the miracle happens around you. You are the miracle—the manifestation. You await this manifestation—and yet you are the manifestation happening right now. Allow this to continue and move through and dissolve the barriers of time and space, of ignorance and fear.

Beloved, be that which you are. You need not do the miracles. You are the miracle. Be that which you are in truth and allow the miracles to happen around you. As you move through barriers, minds and hearts open to the fragrance of joy and love and truth by letting people know that it is all right to be joyous. It is all right to be themselves, it is all right to enjoy and to laugh and to love and to dance and to be the wonder of the universe. Be that which you already are. Do not allow the ego to close down and judge that which it knows nothing of. Love, sing and dance, laugh and live as though there is no other time. Turn each moment into light and joy and you will transcend the will and power of Darkness for evermore.

A crystal is a crystal is a crystal. It is nothing more and cannot be anything less. It can radiate out energy of light—an aura of calm and peace in an otherwise dark and gloomy place. But the crystal can never be more than the crystal or less than a crystal. Its energy can radiate and you and others can open to its radiance and awaken and open the door for your light to radiate out. Where you have been asleep, understand, you can awaken and touch others souls and hearts and minds to open and dance in the light of true understanding, you can never and will never do or be anything other than what you already are. Beloved, realize and awaken to who and what you are—remember.

Dance in the moonlight and dance to the beat of that far away drum and as you touch the sleeping minds, hearts and souls to joy and peace, and new understandings, then, and then only do the miracles you wish to create—materialize. Not by doing, but by your being that which you are.

If you live in your heart and love, you can never, never be hurt again. It is only when you come out of your heart and move into your mind, that you can experience or even know anything other than love. No power or being can move into a heart and make a heart anything other than a heart and love. A broken heart or sad heart is only perceived from outside of the heart, from another point. Move into the heart and dwell in the heart. The heart cannot, will not, ever be anything other than love.

Move into your hearts my friends and be your hearts' desire. Dance with the flow of love and radiate your light into the world of gloom and darkness. Sing out to the world and the voice of love will be heard by all who wish to hear, and shine your light and all who wish to see will see your light and know that when you dwell in light and love—you are light and love. Do not search to do miracles, for whilst you are the centre of light and love, the miracles occur around you as they already have been for years, maybe even lifetimes.

Oh bright light, you cannot and never will see the light you spread for you are the light. You are your miracle—you are the manifestation of love and light and joy in your world of damnation. You are the light—be yourself and allow your light and allow that twinkle—that joy—that laughter—that dance and live and allow people to awaken to their joy.

My passion is to live, love, dance and laugh. Be your passion. You cannot do your passion. Be your passion. We will support you in light and love for evermore. Dance in the wind, the rain and the snow and be the glow and sparkle of life forever more. Love and be always.

The light that shines forth and merges into oneness, no power that comes from without is as strong or ever can be as strong as the power within.

From within is—from the roots of my being, comes strength and power.

My Power

I look at the magnificent ocean in all of its glory and power. I feel the untamed power, and as I watch this wondrous sight, I feel great humility. I realize I can never own the ocean. I acknowledge the great gift of life and of God, and the privilege to be able to stand before the ocean and experience this expansive wonder of the Creator in all of its majesty and feel the energy re-charge and surge through my being. I look at the surrounding hills and the beautiful trees, the clear blue sky; I feel the wind on my face and in my hair and realize I cannot own anything. I see the greatness and the perfection of how everything fits together. For a moment I feel so small and insignificant.

I close my eyes and connect with the wind, the sky, the hills, the trees and the waves of the vast ocean and I understand that my being there is a gift. The Creator even made room and space for me to experience his wonderful vision of perfection, harmony and peace; his masterpiece. Like an insect on an oil painting, I realize that I am not a part of this scenery. I am a guest, free to visit and experience this wonderful planet, but not a part of it. I realize that I am a consciousness that is learning and expanding and as much as I enjoy this beautiful place in which I call home, I can never belong here. Unlike the ocean and the sky and the hills, I am not a permanent fixture. I understand that my place here is only temporary, but I also understand and come to appreciate that this moment in time is mine. I have been given a gift of a few short moments in eternity to experience this wonderful planet and life and it is my choice what I do with those few moments.

This moment I can embrace the power and strength that is all around me. I can choose to make a great attempt at making a difference in this world, for others to see and appreciate the greatness and beauty and opportunity which is on offer, to each and every one of us, or I can choose to remain an insignificant speck like so many that have gone before me and deny the brilliance and magnificence of life and all that it and this planet has to offer. I need to sit quietly and humbly and ask The Great Spirit to give me the inspiration that can inspire me to my greatness. That can help me to accomplish my life destiny that can help me to see my path and the part that I am to play in the unfolding episode of life here on Earth. For there is one thing I am sure of, and that is that God or the Creator did not go to all the trouble to create such a beautiful paradise and bring me here to just be a mere spectator. I know deep within my very being that he needs and wants me to accomplish something. I know that I only need to give it a go, and what I receive out of that will help my being grow and expand from the experience and learn something that just sitting back and letting everyone else do it will never achieve.

I know that even if I fail, he will not judge me and I believe that there is no such thing as failure. For even if I do not succeed at my attempts, what I learn from having a go will help next time I try or will help the next person to succeed. I know that I have a chance to be a part in God's great unfolding plan, and if I don't take the opportunities that present themselves to me, I may miss out altogether. I feel the surge of energy running through my veins and I know I have a purpose and a responsibility to fulfill or else this moment is wasted and is in vain. My being will come and go in but a moment and nothing will have been gained from an opportunity of a lifetime. When will I ever get this moment, this chance again? Maybe never, maybe many times more, who knows?

For now, I need to ponder and listen to my guidance and surrender my ego to the wind, to the spirit within, to God. My heart cries out, *"How may I serve, dear Lord? How may I make a difference? Show me the way?"* Show me the beauty and the greatness of the masterpiece, which we call home, Earth, Life, because we take it for granted. We forget who we are. We forget what we came here for. We fall asleep and pray and ask that someone will come and show us the way, and when they come and attempt to wake us up, we ignore them. We make excuses, we ridicule them, we torture them, and we even kill them, so that we can stay asleep, so that we don't have to do something. How do I fulfil my life's purpose?

The answer sings out from within, *"Live it! Take the opportunity to live each moment—make the most out of this miracle and allow your heart to fly higher and sing the song of joy and peace for evermore."*

God gave us an opportunity to live in a paradise, with the ability to survive, like an emperor or a slave. It is our choice. What you think and believe in this paradise is what you get. If you recognize the gift you have been given and use it to the fullest potential, it will pay great dividends. And if you ignore life and its majesty, and sleep and complain and want someone else to do it for you, then that is what you will create—a nightmare.

At last, I see, I feel, I hear, I know my purpose for being here, which is to remind people of something beyond their wants and desires and to open their hearts and minds to the song of joy. By my living each moment as fully, blissfully and ecstatically as I possibly can, by living life to the fullest, by experiencing every opportunity that is put before me, by enjoying myself to the max, by feeling the feelings, by singing the songs, by walking the journey and by taking a chance.

By cherishing each moment of joy and sorrow and giving thanks for this wondrous moment and opportunity to experience a breath of fresh air. By seeing the Beauty and the Magic in each moment and allow it to touch my heart and my soul, and I can grow beyond the limited vision I have had before. Release my hold on an unreal security and allow myself the freedom to experience each moment I can in this monumental vision of Beauty that the Creator gave to me.

I can feel my freedom and allow myself the scope to fly and should I fail or fall down then I will pick myself up, shake myself off and make another attempt and another until I succeed or until my chance or opportunity or time expires. This time I will succeed by the Grace of God. I give thanks to the Creator and all that is.

Twilight Zone

Twilight Hours is the time spirit sets aside to soar freely through the astral planes. Connecting to people we know and with people and spirit we don't know in this plane. If disturbed suddenly we will find ourselves back in our bodies very quickly, sometimes coming back with a thud or a feeling that we are falling. But we are always connected and it only takes an instant to return. At these times we are connecting with our guides and beings all over the universe and even beyond. We can even do this in times we call daydreaming. We may suddenly be thinking of someone and we connect with them or they are projecting thoughts to us and away we go. This is always best to be used in a positive way. Unfortunately it sometimes can be used in a negative way. Then we are intruding into someone else's space.

Time has no place in the Twilight Zone. The Twilight Zone is a space of absolute freedom. It is like the passageway to astral travel, to travel through different realms. The freedom for our thoughts and beliefs to connect with others' truths, dimensions and realities, Freedom to fly and to delve into the regions of paradise, bringing ecstasy into our own personal worlds. Guard against delving into the past or other peoples' minds for this is an invasion of energy and of privacy. Always show respect.

Time for Gratitude

*H*ow easy is it for us to get all tied up with ourselves that we forget what is really important, like the people who constantly support us whether that be, financially, physically, emotionally, mentally or even spiritually. It seems to me that we are going through a huge lesson of gratitude. How many of us have been grateful for the rain and the water that we take so much for granted. Isn't this a time to become aware of what we have taken for granted? When have you awakened in the morning, went outside and breathed in the fresh new air of a new day and been thankful, that the sun rose and you are alive and able to enjoy your experience of the day. I can guarantee that if you practiced this for a week or two you would begin to see a new life experience, one with enthusiasm, joy and magic. Aren't life's circumstances shouting at us to wake up and to remember what is important in life?

We were looking at the worst drought; other parts of the world are recovering from cyclones, storms, floods, earthquakes, landslides, snowstorms, hurricanes and other unusual weather patterns and disasters. And again another part of the world is recovering from the terror of terrorist activity, and a little further away we have the constant threat that war may break out, and recently the fear of a bird flu pandemic. We have divorce being three times greater expense than weddings. We have Child welfare overworked and the incident of child abuse and all kinds of abuse for that matter at record levels. And until we are involved or directly inconvenienced by these tragedies, we continue on in our daze, only concerned about what directly affects me now. We forget to say, "thank you" to those who go out of their ways to assist us. We forget to have any gratitude for the food that we eat, and for the rain, and for God giving us such a beautiful world for us to graffiti and gradually destroy.

When we can't turn the tap on to get a glass of clean water, will we begin to be grateful for all that we take so much for granted, or will we simply feel hard done by, and start looking for someone else to blame. Perhaps we can blame the government, the council, industry, and the weather, the neighbours or maybe even God. Well if God did it, then maybe we should start to look at why we would deserve such a plight. After all, have we seriously even considered what our world would be like without access to clean water? We would be filthy, sick, starving and life literally would begin to cease. Have you thought about life on Earth without water or are you too busy, surfing the net, or plugged into the ear piece that seems to be almost another organ, these days, too busy making a living or doing what makes you happy?

It's time for us to change things on this planet, and very few of us have a great deal of power to change anything except how we think and how we do things. Perhaps that is enough. Perhaps if we start changing our selves to be a better example, others around us will notice and be encouraged to follow suit. How can we change enough to have an effect, you might ask? Complaining and voicing our concerns are not the way to go, there are enough people complaining and making more noise and feeling important about themselves, but not really getting anything or anyone to change. What if you started saying, "thank you" to the people who matter, before they are not with you anymore? Maybe you could do something to help somebody, and see if they show gratitude to you. Wouldn't that be something nice to experience for a change. Perhaps we could think of ways to do things to save the environment, such as picking up and disposing of rubbish in the correct manner, acting consciously, instead of thinking it's up to someone else's responsibility to change things. Dare to be different and to make a difference, this is how change begins, by acknowledging things that need to change and making an effort. Remember, the most effective way to influence people is to be the way you wish them to be.

Maybe we could write a list of what and who contributes to our world, and consider how we can help the people that matter and contribute to making our world a better place. Maybe we can't make it rain, but we can show God why life on Earth is worthwhile, and begin to take some time to be grateful for the things and people that matter to us. What I really want to say is that we need to look at what we have and be thankful, instead of complaining about what we don't have before we don't even have what we take so easily for granted.

On the subject of gratitude, we probably need to take a good long hard look at ourselves and see where else in our lives a little gratitude would not go astray. Being a medium and channel I get to speak to those passed over and spirit beings, one message always comes through loud and clear, is that they didn't appreciate the time they had here on this plane. When you speak to the elderly, how many say, if only I could do it all over again. We need to look very seriously at ourselves and realize that time is marching on, very rapidly these days and enjoy, and appreciate every moment for every breath we take. We need to appreciate every task that we are able to accomplish, we need to appreciate every experience and every life lesson and live life with gratitude so that we can see where we can accomplish more and have less or no regrets when we are ready to move onto our next level.

Having and showing gratitude for a week or two, will change your life, maybe make it a joy, this maybe the recipe to saving our world.

The Essence of Love

Be balanced and centred in life knowing and trusting that the Love of God is flowing through you and Life is unfolding lovingly in the way in which it is meant to, just for you.

One Man
One God
One Religion

*I*n these times, we are given many opportunities to look around and say, *"What is going on?"* We speak of unity, being one and being at one, and we look at our fellow man and judge him and ask, *"How can I be a part of him or her? I am nothing like that. This is not me."* And yet when we go within and meditate and we search our hearts and our souls, and if we can be honest we may come to the conclusion that: Yes this person who is before us is indeed a part of us. They are showing us a beautiful part of ourselves, and if we find it difficult to see the beauty, then maybe they are showing us a part of ourselves that we need to look at. Bring to the surface, forgive and heal this part of ourselves and integrate into our consciousness to bring us to a wholeness and appreciation of which we really are. Instead of our ego and pride going into denial and stating, *"I am not like that, it has nothing to do with me, I am better, I don't and I won't accept such nonsense."*

Search a little deeper, be a little more open, and be more honest, *"Maybe there is something there that this person is mirroring back to me. Yes I see, in that instance, maybe I was doing what this person is showing me now."* Sometimes it is hard to admit when we are wrong, or that we could have behaved or reacted a little differently. To admit that we are not right or perfect takes away our righteousness. It denies our egotistical boasts and claims. Yes, now I understand, now I see me, this is me. Now I can forgive and accept that person and forgive and accept myself, once again I am in union with myself, and God. I am one with mankind and—I see love.

If just for a moment, we were able to grasp, the concept that there is only one of us here. There is only one time, there is only one God, there could and would only be one religion and that is Love.

There is only one time, which is now and is this moment. Everything happens now, in this moment and can only happen now and in this moment. Allow your mind to relax and settle into this moment. Forget and release the past for it is not real anymore, you understand according to your experiences, you may see the past one way and others see it from a whole different perspective, so how can it be real? Release your expectations and desires for a future that may or may not eventuate and bring all of your awareness into this moment, here and now because this is where your power is, in the present. This is where and how you can make the best choices and life changing decisions and you will have more clarity than ever before. Be present, be spontaneous, be here and in this moment. You cannot make choices in the past, nor can you make choices in the future. Accept this wonderful gift of life called the present now and live fully and joyfully in each moment, see the beauty that is before you and watch as your world transforms and changes with excitement and wonderment every day.

There is one God, God is the life, the breath and the light, the life force that is in everything. There is God or there is not. Show me what is not—no, you cannot. God is in everything. See God in this moment of time. You may pray to Jesus, Buddha, Angels, Ascended Masters, Prophets, but they will only show you the way to God. God is the ultimate. God is all.

So we have one man or woman who sees him or herself mirrored in everything and in every way. We have one moment of time, which is now, and we have one God, which is in everything. There can be no other conclusion than there should be one religion which is what God is, which is Love. How simple would life be if there was one religion, with one principle?

'Love God Now!'

When we interpret this: Love means to like, adore, be with, encourage, and joy, beauty, peace, and bliss. God is everything—. It is you; and me and existence. Now is the only time. One would only have to ask the following three questions:

"Is this Love?

Is this God?

Is this now?"

Can your mind imagine living for now, loving and being with God, because if Heaven was to be on Earth, this would be the new religion in all of its entirety.

Blessings from Ur

Peace On Earth

We all pray and believe we want peace on Earth. And yet, how many of us have peace in our own lives, our own families and homes, not to mention ourselves. What is peace? Perhaps it is contentment, an inner feeling that everything is okay and even though changes may come and go we will be okay. I guess in order to find peace, we need to have balance. A balanced perception of how things are meant to be and not how we think they should be.

I believe that in order to find peace, we need to dissolve some of our expectations, of ourselves as well as what we expect from other people. If there were no expectations of others, we couldn't be disappointed if what we expect doesn't arrive or comes in a different form to what we had wanted. An expectation, both of ourselves and of others, leads to pressure, and pressure is a quick way to disrupt our balance and equilibrium in life. When pressure builds around us and builds within ourselves, we need to find a loving way to release it, before it causes ill health or malfunction in our relationships with others and within our own body and mind.

Sometimes simply stepping out of the situation for a short time can eliminate the pressure. Long enough to see what is actually happening without the pressure of built up emotions and expectations to perform or to give or do. Sometimes, we become so caught up in our scenarios that we can't see or even think clearly and then we either explode or resort to pure stubbiness, or implode and cut ourselves off from those around the situation and us. By this time, the basic problem is long gone and smothered by a multitude of other scenarios. One thing leads to another and before we know it, world war or a domestic argument has broken out, either in the world outside or in the world that we live in.

Chaos can erupt in associations, work colleagues, friends, our families, or even in our own heads and realities. And before we know it, we have experienced, judged, crucified and buried wonderful friends and or family members without a word of communication.

Our egos, our personalities have a lot to answer for, don't they? Well, enough of how things can get out of hand, we all know these moments of grief that erupt from time to time. Let's talk about solutions, how to resolve these issues when they arise. Acceptance is a wonderful key. We don't have to like, agree or enjoy any others' perceptions, way or belief, just accept that everybody has a right to an opinion and they don't need to justify their perceptions anymore then we need to defend ours. People can stand their ground, stand in their power and be themselves and be true to themselves as much as they wish, so long as they realize they don't have the right to stand on other people. To abuse others rights, or take away others power in so doing. Those are usually the first words declared in open warfare.

Remember we are empowered spiritual beings, capable of doing anything except when it interferes with another. Because when it does, this means we are going to enter into a conflict and if we persist and take over and squash the more timid or softer people, Karma will prevail. Then we will experience what we have put upon others. This is why Jesus said, "Turn the other cheek," and "Do unto others as you would have them do unto you." This is the law of karma and of life, and being a Universal Law, which will never change at any time ever. Remember there are wheels; (or cycles—within cycles), and things always come round eventually.

If we want peace, drop your rights and wrongs and accept that everything will balance out if we allow it. Allowing is a lovely word that is very different to control, manipulate or manoeuvre. If you want peace you must live your life in a peaceful and loving way.

If anyone is suffering from anxiety, a simple cure for relaxing tension and anxiety which leads to a build up of pressure is to simply enjoy what we are doing, where we are living, who we are living and working with. We all have desires and dreams, goals and wishes of greatness and abundance. Peace begins when you acknowledge and accept that you are that which you are. Whatever you have or are doing right now, whoever you are with, enjoy them or what you are doing or where you are. Be peaceful. Be peaceful within and the outside world will mirror the inside and you will find peace.

Miracles

My friend Neville asked me the question; *"Judy, what do you think Love is?"* I felt my reply was inadequate, but the more I think of my answer, the more I like it. Freedom; is being happy with oneself, detached and without expectation, sharing with another, and so on.—But with the following answer, it became clearer, most felt that Love is pain or causes or leads to pain.

And I say unto you, 'love is not pain'. Pain is pain, separation is pain, and mind is pain. I believe Love is sweet; Love is strength, endurance, and understanding, loyalty and peace.

Pain is pain. Separation is pain!

Love is union, oneness, and wholeness—It is Freedom!!!

When we love another, we come together in a union, whether it be by conception, birth, friendship, partnership or; marriage. Union; God is union, God is Love, God is whole. When we leave another, this is not love. This is separation, which causes pain. Leaving a loved one because of arguments, circumstances, travel, divorce, death, is separation, which causes pain and suffering. This is pain.

If we stay in Love and the other departs, no matter which level, travel, home, town, new path, death, we can still connect throughout the heart and psychically and still be in touch with that person eternally. This is how we can come back together from past lives and people who have moved away from each other reunite after many years even in the same lifetime.

We went into a meditation session and met with Merlin. We were invited to ask questions, So questions I asked. What is the meaning of life? Answer—To experience the wonder, the mystery, to learn and grow from these experiences, to expand our consciousness and our beings. The more one experiences, the more opportunity there is to grow.

'How do you find Love?'

By being myself, and by loving my being and myself, my uniqueness and this is what Jesus meant when he said, *"love thyself."* And then you can love others for whom and what they are. And this is Love.

Understanding, that each person is an individual with a world of possibilities, choosing to be with you at any given time. Appreciate the miracle of existence and the people who are choosing to spend time with you. By being myself and by loving my being. Throw away the masks, the facades and false personalities. These are imposters and will not sustain. If you act anyway other than being true to yourself, you will come undone. If you don't like yourself, than change what you are at the core level and act with integrity and truth. Better to be disliked for who you are, than liked for who you are not, because when something happens and you can't hide behind the mask, the illusion anymore, you will be liked even less as a liar or a cheat or an imposter.

This is what it means to love YOU! Develop the qualities that you do like. Practice them until they resonate and become natural to you, or do the work and release resentments and entanglements that keep us from being everything that we truly are. Dare to be yourself at all costs. Then if someone is attracted to you, they will be there for the right reasons. This is what is called being true to you.

How do I create the miracles that I have been told I will create?

By believing you can. By wanting something to materialize and believing you have the power and deserve them. By needing the outcome to happen or else it will fail.

Not by wishing. When you wish, you think it is unlikely. You think that it would be nice, but probably wouldn't happen, for instance, "wishing to win lotto!" You know that it is a fair chance that you may not win, but you wish you would. If you don't, then you know that there will be another solution, no matter how badly you could use the money from a lottery win. You have created the possibility of a miracle happening, by creating lotto. For example, when I was young, a bank manager told my intended husband that we should invest in his bank, that he would see to it that when we wanted a home loan, he would make sure we could get one. We were paying off a block of land and in our estimation we could easily afford to pay of a house loan. But when we went to the bank, the manager told us we needed two thousand dollars more in assets, or even if we could get a loan of another two thousand dollars, he could approve the loan. Sitting in his office feeling horribly dejected and as if we had failed for all time, I prayed and wished that my mother could win the casket and lend us the two thousand dollars. I believed with all my heart and soul that she was the only person I knew who deserved to win the money and would lend it to me. We left his office with his assurance that should we find the money he would help us. When we arrived at my home, a bank manager from another bank was congratulating my mother for having won the Golden Casket Draw. This was a true story and a true miracle.

You create opportunities for miracles constantly. But you don't believe they will happen for you. You don't believe in the magic of the universe that it can manifest, just as you want it to. It is your doubt that blocks you from creating miracle after miracle. Miracles equal no doubt. Have you ever seen a magician that was not confident? No, he believes he can.

Believe that you are the magician, channelling the energy that does create miracles. Mountains, whether they are made of emotion, overwork or ignorance, or even the real thing can and will be moved when the right energy is placed there. Be the channel and watch your world transform into wonderment with new experiences creating opportunities of joy, laughter, love and expansion on all levels.

Be the magician by being the master of your life, by taking responsibility for all of your creations and dealing with them in a positive way. Enjoy every opportunity to transform negative situations into positive and moving forward into your empowerment. Create your miracles as you channel your creative energy.

I Can Fly

There comes a time in everyone's life, when we need to stop, look, listen and assess the past. Know that the past experiences have brought you to who you are now. Through enduring tests and building strength to overcome obstacles and enjoy the experience of success and the joy of love and the disappointments and trials of relationships and things not going the way we want them to. We have experienced, learnt and grown from many different people and situations in our life. Sometimes things have gone the way we thought they would and wanted, sometimes even better and sometimes not that way at all. In times of fear and doubt, how often have things turned out for the better? In times of great expectation or opportunity, how often has the outcome been greater or lesser than what we thought would be the outcome? How did these experiences affect us? Did they?

Did bitter disappointments make us angry, feel victimized, and contribute to making us feel disillusioned and give us an attitude that the world owes us something. Or did we watch the experience, knowing and trusting that this is an opportunity to learn and grow and move into our centre. Trust and have faith and knowledge that something was happening for ours or someone else's greater good. Maybe a change was occurring and that it would ultimately move us into another situation and opportunity, even better than our previous expectations allowed. For instance, when we've been working hard, hoping to achieve some reward or recognition or even stability and mastering some ability and suddenly we are told our services are no longer required, or the company closes down or moves, or situations arise which make us feel we need to move on. Doesn't more often than not a new and even more enjoyable job or opportunity present itself?

How often, down the track, do we sit back and think, *"Yes, they actually did us a favour. Now I am so much better off."* And yet at the time it feels like, we are out of control, everything and everyone is against us. God and the angles have forgotten us and we are totally alone and totally a victim of some mad mind who loves to punish us instead of rewarding us. 'Nothing ever goes right! Nobody ever helps me! I am so tired of being unappreciated. I did my best, but it is never good enough.' And on it goes. Can you relate to these feelings of despair? I can, I have, and yet now I know and have proved that no matter what falls out of my life, something better follows.

What if you had married your childhood sweetheart? We look back and think how sweet those times were, but surely if we had married them, our marriage may have fallen down the gurgler, obviously or else why didn't you? Every time my life crumbles, I ask what can I learn from this, how can I grow?

I wait to see what happens. When people shift and change their attitudes toward me and it feels like our friendship, relationship is leaving my life, I know that I have helped them as much as I can. I also know that they have helped me as much as they can and it's time to love them and let them go. For, if I were to hold on to them, I am going to feel pain. This pain is because I am split—part of me is with them and not here with me. I may become scattered, fractured, angry and hurt. That is my choice. The other choice is to stay centred, send and radiate love and light and let them go. This comes back to respect, respecting their choices and their journey. If that special person leaves, then stay with self, nurture self and love self. They have gone, if they chose to move on, and you understand that you need to stay whole and wait for the next experience or person to unfold in your life.

People and situations arise in our lives so that we can learn more about ourselves. Greater challenges bring greater fears to the surface. Parts of us we didn't know existed, need to surface in order to heal and to overcome more difficult situations and repeat until we have mastered that particular lesson. How did you handle that last outburst or disappointment?

Know and understand that you, have by now either flowered and grown or, have become bitter and resentful. This is your choice. You are not your experiences. You are not the past, even though the past has brought you to whom you are now. Can you let go of someone you love, and continue loving them and wish them well on their journey, or will you try to hold on and pull yourself apart and be fractured and resent that they are no longer a part of your world. Nobody else can make you happy, happiness like peace, comes from within yourself.

This is what I have learned this past life. Enjoy each new experience and person that enters your life and make the most out of every situation, because either I may move on or for whatever reason, or they may move on. I may never have the opportunity to laugh with or cry with this person again.

Every time I meet someone I don't like, I meet a part of me that needs more of my love, understanding and nurturing. This person is showing me an aspect of myself that I don't love or maybe not even aware of. This part of me has emerged for me to understand an even greater and vaster experience of love. You may ask how can I love a liar, a cheat, a thief, a rapist or even a murderer? This is not a part of me. No? Let's see.

When you meet a liar, someone who obviously doesn't tell the truth, ask yourself, *"Where am I lying to myself in my life. Am I fooling myself and believing something that in truth is not so?"* Be honest, when did you make up excuses to get out of something and then be let down by someone else also trying to get out of a similar situation. The Law of Karma states what you put out; you must also experience, because this world is like a mirror, a reflection of self. If you don't like what you see, you need to do something from within, you can't change the reflection. If you do your best, are honest and loving and stand in truth and integrity, you will always see something of beauty; no matter how hard the lessons or your life becomes.

If you are robbed, then look at where you have taken or kept something that rightfully belongs to another. Or look at what you are holding onto that you need to let go of. If we are busy holding on, we have no hands free to receive anything else that the universe wishes to endow upon us.

If our cup is full, we can't fill it anymore. Let it all go, so that something or someone else can fill the void, thankfully, not too many of us meet up with rapists or murderers in our lifetime. Remember we may wish to justify many traits in our psyche that we are not honest enough or capable of dealing with yet. And be careful of judging people to harshly or cruelly, for as you judge, you shall be judged. The American Indians had a saying; you cannot judge a man until you have walked a mile in his moccasins. Sometimes the tests and trials become so harsh that we don't handle things as well as we would even like to. Situations arise and we act severely or without discernment, but maybe sometimes this happens to teach someone else a lesson.

So back to my time, to assess my past experiences, this part of my life to date has taught me the truth in what I have shared thus far. As much as my experiences have taught me, shown me, and helped me to progress, I am not those experiences. I am not the past, nor the people that have helped me to progress. Even though they are showing me parts of my being, my patterns and beliefs, and helping me to expand on my boundaries and consciousness, they are not me. My personality, the way I relate to people and situations and the way I perceive experiences, my actions, my reactions, my pain and sorrow and even my joy and happiness is not me.

For instance, someone says to me, *"Judy, you are fat and ugly!"* I can retaliate with all kinds of insults and aggression. The fat and ugly may or may not be true, but they are not me. My fat and my ugliness do not feel insulted. I choose to feel insulted. I decide that fat and ugly is bad, an insult. This is my judgement. My judgement, my insults and my aggression are not me. That may be the way I choose to react to someone's observation, but they are not me and it is only in my mind that I see fat and ugly as an insult or rejection. This may not even be the case.

When someone else comes and tells me I am beautiful and perfect just the way I am, the hurt and pain dissolves, and I may now be experiencing joy and happiness, which is also not me.

So who am I?—Who am I?

I know I am not the experience, I am not pain or the feeling I choose to experience, then who am I? I am not the victim or the victimizer. I am not the career, the success, the failure, the disappointment or the ecstasy.

I am consciousness. When my pain goes, I don't disappear. When my joy goes, I don't disappear. When my career as a nurse, banker, painter, artist or mother goes, I am still here. When I am sleeping, I am still here. When my relationship ends, I am still here. When my body dies and drops away, I am still here. When this world as I know changes and ends, I am still here. When my arms and legs are amputated, I am still here. When my bank balance is overdrawn I am still here. When the sun sets, I am still here. No matter how depressed and miserable I choose to feel or how happy and jubilant I can be, I am still here. For eternity I am still here. The greatest teachings say to me that I am love, but when I love, I am here. But when my loving turns to hatred and disappointment and disillusionment,—I am still here.

Maybe it is time to begin to love myself, because no matter how many lives I live, or try to hide in, or bodies I live in, I am still here. Jobs may come and jobs have gone. People have come and people have gone. Friendships and relationships have come and gone. Lives have come and lives have gone. I have come but have never gone. I am here present now, and there is no other time except now.

It is time to assess my life, my existence thus far.

What have I experienced?

I am an author; I wrote this article, I wrote poetry, so I'm a poet and didn't know it. I have told jokes so I am a comedian. I have drawn and painted pictures, an artist that makes me. I have strummed a guitar, a musician by far. I have built sandcastles in the sand, and houses, that makes me a builder. I have taught and learnt so much; that makes me a student and a teacher. I am a mother and a daughter, I have been in service and I have been to the bank, which makes me a banker. I have invested money and time, which makes me an investor. I have learned to use computers and how to arrange flowers; I am a minister of religion and marry people. I sold and made waterbeds; I distributed Amway, juice and Tupperware. I made pottery and sold hand made goods. I am a new age consultant, counsellor and therapist. I have achieved everything that my mind has imagined and more. I am still breathing and have money in the bank. This makes me successful. I have many gifts, talents and accomplishments.

What do I need to do now? What will I choose to achieve now? I am aware my life has been filled and is about to empty and be experienced from another consciousness. I am now in choice, where do I go from here?

I take responsibility for my choices and as I sit and ponder at my next adventure, I give thanks for all of my gifts and all that I have achieved, for all the beauty in the world, for all my friends and loved ones and for those who love me. For everything that I see before me, I am immensely grateful for and appreciate that through all of my experiences and opportunities, I have come to learn and know the Truth.

Whilst sitting on this mountain, waiting for the next opportunity to come to me, or sitting and pondering about my next adventure. When my job as a clairvoyant changes and ends and my joy and pride disappear, and I am left wondering what I shall do next, I am still here. What do I choose next? Where do I go from here? What once fulfilled, challenged and rewarded me, no longer fulfils or interests me. So it must change, but into what?

As I sit in this space of achievement and knowing, I am ready to move on. I ponder over what I have achieved and choose my next challenge, my next path or journey. I search for the next goal and make plans of how I will go about achieving success. I need to know what it takes to become my next goal, so that my journey can begin to unfold to accomplishment. I need to take into consideration my resources, my needs, my abilities and limitations and what I wish to achieve and to gain out of the experience. Then carefully travel down the mountain and follow the path and stay true to my cause, my goal.

Or should I attempt the greatest adventure yet known to my consciousness? Should I walk to the end of this path, the very cliff edge, and jump into the abyss, taking only my trust and faith and my consciousness? If I jump, will I fall down or will I learn to fly?

The Rainbow

S ome people may say that I live in a dream, always chasing rainbows. As I lay in a semi-trance state of being, holding on to the golden cross with crystals placed in it and heart shaped intrusions, I followed the path to a crystal cave. This time, I was taken deep into a cave on a mine carriage. It felt like, I needed to go through one of the heart shaped doorways to begin this journey. Travelling on the mine carriage, I was reminiscing, thinking that everybody thinks that I live in my own mystical world, half off the planet, chasing rainbows. Believing in the best in people, believing in love, believing in miracles, and that we can create a beautiful world. My heart began to open more and more, as my companion looked at the rock walls in this cave and showed me that they were smooth and glistened of golden fleck as the light gleamed on them as we went deeper into what seemed a mine shaft. The strange thing was that we were going higher, not lower. My companion reminded me that all that glistens and sparkles is not gold.

We eventually pulled up into a room filled with golden light. Everything changed to golden amber. I filled my being with this golden amber light and energy. It reminded me of the story called the Midas touch. Where the king asked to be given the gift of the Midas and everything he touched turned to gold—everything. Including his daughter, and he was pleased when the gift, which he then believed to be a curse was removed. He wished for that gift for the wrong reasons. He was filled with greed, vanity and negative egotistical pursuits of wealth and power for all the wrong reasons, for his own greed, for his own abusive power and benefits.

I was then shown what I would be able to use this gift of golden energy and touch for. If I can look and touch a person and bring them joy, health, hope, faith, love, if I can help a person to believe in him or herself, if I can give a person the courage to go on just one more day, than I have used my gift wisely. If a person comes to see me and they leave with a little insight, a little stronger, a little lighter, with a glimmer of hope, then I am using this gift the right way. I am sharing this gift and helping to make a better world. They showed me that I could change the way I do readings a little, not so much predicting the future in truth as it stands now, but to focus more on how it can be better. Show them how their world can transcend from doom and gloom, to something with hope and faith, instead of just truth as I perceive it, but by sharing trust and faith.

This is the dawn of the golden age, where darkness, gloom and negative aspirations are transformed into light, courage, and strength through the will of God, through trusting in the power of the light. What have we got to lose? Everything negative and then through the law of god, everything which is taken away will be replaced with something of equal or greater power. If right now, we stop listening to the press, stop hearing the talk of war, anger and fear. If we sat right at this moment, became still and quiet and prayed, we can pray for peace, for the light of God to transcend all the negativity in peoples' minds and thought patterns and make this a world, a place of grace and glory. But we need to believe that God will hear us. We need to believe that the angelic kingdom understands that it is really peace and love that our hearts, minds and souls long for and wishes to experience. We need to know and understand that if we ask God for something that he will move heaven and earth to make it happen for us. And we need to be given the opportunity to experience our part in it. Not leave it all up to God and let him click his fingers, like changing a television channel. Oh today we have fear of world war—click—tomorrow we'll have peace and goodwill. No! It doesn't work like that. We can already do that in our own lives, our own worlds, in our own living rooms. We can move from the stories of hatred, disillusionment, torment and fear, which excite us into believing war is our only option on the world news.

Then flick with the click of a button to be deeply entranced in someone's' greatest love, romance and drama story of the century, to a documentary on how mosquitoes multiply and so on. One doesn't learn anything from that experience, except knowledge of what may or may not be truth, or someone else's perception of truth. No people, mankind needs to take responsibility and acknowledge they created the state the world is in now. Through greed and lusting after materialism and power for their own benefits and egos, by only focusing on what they want, they're own needs, not for helping people and for the greater good of the community. It is time we realized how powerful we are, and instead of fearing the worst, or believing in our power for our own selfish ambitions and materialistic gains, we need to pull together and believe that as a community we can turn this world around. We can make this world a peaceful loving society, which cares for and takes responsibility for the weak and encourages and supports our strong leaders instead of ridiculing them and trying to bring them down.

If someone tries to advance, support them or at least be open to what they have to offer, and if you have a better idea, voice it, don't just sit back and add negativity and say, *"that won't work"*. If you feel you can do a better job, get up and do it, or do something about it instead of allowing everybody else to do it for you, and then sitting back and complaining that nobody ever does anything or that everything is done wrong. Be positive, take positive steps, and write a letter, an article, start a group but do something positive.

It begins like this. Every morning, we wake up; thank God, the angels, and the higher realms for keeping us safe through the night. We thank Mother Earth and the nature spirits, for giving us a solid foundation, the Earth to live on and appreciate and see its natural beauty. We give thanks and ask our guides, the masters of light to lead us and show us a wonderful day, so that we can experience and share in the miracle of living a life of beauty and good will.

The first day or week, month or even year, you may need to reinforce this constantly, but like any negative pattern, through perseverance, repetition and faith it works and will change your life. When the kids play up and don't want to go to school, maybe, you need to take a minute out, breathe and thank God for them being there. How sad would you be if they suddenly weren't there anymore? Give thanks for their health and vitality and fun loving ways.

When you go to the office or your work and you are confronted with reams of work, or complaints or equipment failing to operate, take a minute out, breathe and thank God for your job, for the abundance of work and money it brings you, for being able to help sort someone's confusion out. Give 'thanks,' what would it be like if all of a sudden there were no jobs. If you don't like your job, see if there is something you would be happier doing. Create your world the way you want it and give thanks for everything you receive. Don't be a victim in any circumstance, realize, that you have the power to change your world. All that you need do is believe that you can. Understand, you created your situations, your life, your experiences, if you are bored or in a situation you don't like experiencing, thank God for the lessons you have learnt and the experience and set about to change it to what you want to experience next. Your choice—You decide.

So after chasing rainbows for years and probably lifetimes upon lifetimes, I believe I've found my proverbial 'pot of gold'. It is not great physical wealth, for in the past I have had glimpses of all the glory, and happiness that excessive money brings. And what it creates as well; also the jealousy, the betrayals, the responsibilities and dilemmas that wealth brings. The need to protect, and to hold on to it so that it doesn't dwindle away or that someone doesn't cheat you out of it. Whatever energy it takes to create money or wealth, it takes at least double and maybe more to hold on to it.

No; it is abundance, but not money or wealth. It isn't even that great love, that perfect partner, 'the one'; no it is the greatest love of all. The love of oneself, me, at last I am whole, I am one and in harmony with spirit, my purpose, my being. I am at peace with who I am and with God. This is the pot of gold at the end of the rainbow. This is where it is to be found. Where I am whole and I don't need anyone or anything to give me happiness than what I have right this moment. And I know that everything else will flow from this place of pure love and light, and I know I will have to keep working on myself constantly to maintain this space of love and freedom. Love of God and myself and the freedom to be myself, no matter what anybody else thinks of me or what they say, for I have found a place of peace and contentment that is beyond anything in the material world or anybody's judgements. I know that I come from a place deep within the heart, steeped in compassion, love and beauty and I see all these things in the world around me and I see the beauty in everything before me.

When something good in my life ends, it shows me, it is time to move on to another experience, something better than before. When situations fall down and causes pain, it shows me a part of myself that I need to heal and to love and to be nurtured. When people criticize and condemn me, it shows me a part of them that needs to love themselves more, a belief of theirs that sees something threatening that they fear, will bring change and growth to their consciousness. Wherever I am, I can easily see the beauty or the light, and if for a second, I forget, I fall asleep, I become separated, then something deeper than ever before is about to surface, that I can heal and learn and grow from. But now I look for the light, for the lesson and realize that this is something my soul wishes me to experience. So that I can become even more than I was before, this time my beliefs, my knowing tells me that, *"this too shall come to pass,"* and how I handle this situation is my choice. Whether I choose to love the experience and grow from it or fear it and become a victim to it is really my choice, but also determines the quality of the next experience. Whether I indeed learn from it and grow or choose to repeat it again until I do learn and grow from it is also my choice.

And now I see and understand why the journey has appeared to get harder as we get higher or further into spiritual awakening. Because the veil, the block, that hides the truth from us, is of our own making. We put it there, because we believed or we were conditioned to believing that we could find something more, somewhere else or in someone else instead of in our own self. We believed that the grass is always greener someplace else, we believed in someone else, we believed that someone else could be more, have more, and we forgot that everything we need is right there, within us. Every opportunity is right there before us. What do I want to do next? All I need do is decide, set about being interested in what that is, study it, learn about it and go and do it. And while I love doing it, I will continue to do it; and if my heart is not in it than it will fail or I will move onto the next experience, and I have the power and the freedom to know and to do just that.

This is my pot of gold at the end of the rainbow. To know what love is, and to know that there is an equal power other than love, and that is my mind *"ego"*—fear. I can communicate and believe in the angels of heaven or give my power to the demons and devils of fear and hell. I can walk tall, strong and in my power, in the light, in truth and in justice. Or I can engage in the games of people's egos and be seduced by want and desire. And if I am not aware, become entrapped in the forces of darkness and evil and stop living my life to become someone else's pawn to be manipulated and take my role as victim. Every moment I am in choice, I choose my experience, whether I come from love or fear. Whether I am a victim or walk in truth and stare fear straight in the eyes and know it can never hurt me unless I let it. If I love myself, even when everyone else chooses to deny me of what is mine and seems against me. If I come from integrity and honesty and I work for the greatest good of all by realizing that I am the all; that everything else is a manifestation of what is within me, then I am free to be love. Then, I am free. At last I am free to be me.

Journey to the Light

Fairy I once was

Till one day I was given a choice

And then I became a butterfly

Transformation from chrysalis to caterpillar

And then

To butterfly representing Freedom

I brought the magic with me

On my journey to the Light

So that I could transform

The ugly and the dim to beauty and bright

Bringing life and magic to all

The creatures great and small

On my journey home, toward the light

Then one day the magic rained

Upon a Golden hue

And the light came down and

Said to me

"It's time, at last—you're home."

The Hand of God

May the hand of God support your universe, and may you trust and believe that God, whatever you perceive God to be, as your saviour, your protector and your guide. I believe that one of the biggest confusions in the world even to this day is in regards to who and what is God. If we can know who and what God is, then we can perceive our place in the world in relation to God and to everyone else as well for that matter, and even to ourselves. However, we can only get to know God through getting to know ourselves and loving who we are. This sounds like a cliché', but in truth it is real and only what is real sustains. This is the reason our world, our lives, keep changing, because in a way, they are not real. "Life is an illusion." Yesterday! How do we go about proving yesterday even existed? Your yesterday was a whole different scenario to my yesterday, even if we had spent the whole day together.

The only way to measure yesterday or any pre-existence for that matter is to look to what we have brought from our past. If you look at your belongings, (objectively), you will see what you value in life. If you look at your partner, friends and family, you will see yourself. Sometimes we don't like what we see. Persevere, because we won't recognize anything we don't know ourselves. Our personalities, our belongings, are who we really are. For instance, if we love saxophone music, we may own a saxophone, or at least a miniature one, a picture of a sax or some great artist playing one, a CD of blues music etc. We are drawn to collect and keep memorabilia that constitutes what we like or are drawn too.

When we can understand and know ourselves, who we are, we can then form a relationship and an understanding of God and begin to see God and Godliness in each other and in the world around us.

It is true, if you change one small perception, you will change your whole world and possibly the people in your world, or at least your perception to people and to life and this is what Enlightenment, or Awakening and awareness is all about. It is changing your view, your judgements, your perceptions, your beliefs and your understandings. It is accepting that nothing will change if we do not make the effort to change the inside of ourselves first, by trusting your knowing, your deep gut knowing you are going to begin to reach a fundamental understanding of who or what God is and your relationship with the creator.

Religions is a way to knowing God. God does not reside in any church, synagogue, or chapel, or ashram or centre, anymore than in your own home or whatever you feel is sacred. When we can't or don't have the comprehension and enlightenment to understand and know God, then we were able to put our trust and faith in someone or something that did, or said they did. For instance; the great teachers, and masters, such as; Jesus, Buddha, Krishna and so on, the great teachers who were enlightened, who did meet with and know God, who showed compassion to us, who tried to show us the way to God, to enlightenment, to God Realization. But for most of us, we didn't understand or comprehend their messages, we thought that God was an outside person, separated from us. We were and are left in the dark. The dark is being unknowing, disconnected, separated and maybe even lost. When left in the dark, locked up in a dark room for instance, we may pray for light, we may pray for understanding, we may pray or cry out for someone to come and save us and open the door to freedom; to knowledge, to knowing and to understanding.

These saviours are the great teachers, they did come, and they opened the door, they shone the light of knowing, understanding of love and compassion and even forgiveness, but we could not fully arise to their level of understanding. We didn't want to do all the hard work of changing our reality, changing our beliefs. We didn't want to understand that by changing our perceptions, by changing our beliefs and who we believed we were, and by letting the past go and who we thought we were for lifetimes, we would empower ourselves. We wanted to let these teachers do it for us. We praised and believed in the teachers and we believed them to be gods and goddesses. We didn't listen closely to them, because they said, "I am the way, I am the light" not that they were God, anymore or any less than you or I are God. When we refused to make the changes and follow the example they set, by letting go of our old beliefs and patterns of behaviour, we blamed them for our plight, and cursed our saviours, our angels, our teachers for not what they did but for what we did not do.

How easy is it to believe that Jesus, Buddha, Krishna and so on can live our lives for us? That they can heal us and save us, can make us have complete and have wholesome lives, and make us who we were always intended to be, rich, famous and healthy. And if we are not all that we think we would like to be, we cry out, "why have you forsaken me, in my time of need!" No, they cannot do it for us, they can tell us how to do it, they can show us the way, but we have to do something in order to receive the benefits, we have to make the required changes, not think that they can do it for us. It is not enough to praise them or to put them on a pedestal and expect that because we believe in them; Jesus, or Buddha, or Krishna, or any great teacher or saint that the work is done and they will save us from hell and damnation. They came to show us how to be as they are, as they have achieved, we can too.

The fifth principle in the principles of Spiritualism is *"Personal Responsibility"*, which will lead us to enlightenment if we practice it, practice taking responsibility for our own thoughts, our choices and our decisions in our lives. How easy is it to have false Gods and idols and place our dependence onto someone else or on the church or on religion? How easy is it to blame everyone else and everything else for all of our own inequities instead of being responsible for ourselves and our own lives?

Personal Responsibility means, **I am** responsible for who I am and for what I create and co-create. I am responsible for my creations, for my belongings, for my beliefs and my whole life. I chose this incarnation to play a part in the great unfoldment of this world to give me the opportunity of living out my identity, who I am in whatever way I choose. It is my choice. And when I look at who I am and what I have created, I can decide if I love it as it is or I can continue to grow and to change some more.

How much more fun is it to grow in the light, in freedom, than to be locked up in a dark cage, which is within our own mind and thoughts? Any of the great teachers and teachings will lead you to the door. You and only you can take the steps to move out of that dark cage and expand your consciousness enough to dwell in the light. You are the one who has to knock.

The Light of God is so bright, so warm and so loving, even overpowering after having been locked away in the dark for an extended period of time, which could be days, years or even lifetimes. At times, we may think we want to stay there because we have forgotten and we may even fear the light and we may feel safer in our old comfort zone, where it is cold and dark and we can revel in being the victim. Oh poor me, oh woe is me, where everything has happened to me and against me, where it is not my fault, where I am happy to blame someone else. It is everyone else's fault and besides others are doing things to me and the circumstances aren't right, I can revel in being the King or Queen of my dark old castle.

Let the dark old castle fall. The Tower in the Tarot suggests that when our old beliefs, old patterns, old ways of doing things, old understandings and associations shatter, we should let them fall away and stand up tall and in the light of our new found understandings. Look at your fears, one by one. There is nothing to fear except fear itself. We have fears such as the fear of being successful, the fear of being alone, the fear of losing, the fear of being new, the fear of being? Be successful, it won't hurt, it will empower you and strengthen you. In being alone, you will be surprised how many friends you will gain. Lose what you hold onto, you will see how much more comes to you. Be new, forget the old, become uplifted, energized and excited about life.

There are no boogiemen, only the thoughts we feed ourselves, to feed our fears. Become responsible, face up to your fears and step out of your old fragmented ways and enjoy the comfort and security and love of the creator and all the power you choose to drawer to you to live a happy and comfortable life. Then love will make sense in all of its wonderment.

The Conclusion

*W*ell folks, it is the beginning of another new year and soon it will be Easter and so on, but wait; no, it is the end of 2012, the end of the world as we knew it, the end of the Mayan Calendar. It seems to me that as we move into 2013 and into the new Chinese Year of the Snake, there is a strange new vibration. People all over the world have been stretched into all kinds of shapes and sizes, dealing with all kinds of tests and hardships in regards to careers, finances and relationships over the past several years. I was once told when I went through my gruesome divorce many years ago that all relationships that for want of a better way of saying it, weren't made in heaven would have to split or end. Well, I think that time of testing and reshaping us in our relationships and in all facets of our lives, is practically over. Except of course when we move blindly into something that sadly reminds us of some fairy tale, which of course maybe happy in the beginning.

I believe there is a subtle new energy moving into our space that gives us a new responsibility about making rash decisions. It encourages us to look before we leap and yet it also encourages us to take steps forward with discernment and not to miss out on opportunities of fulfilling our life paths and purposes. I expect to see much more movement and advancement on all levels in the coming year or two. Many spiritually gifted people previously wanted to move ahead and create centres and retreats, only to meet closed doors and blocked paths. I believe soon we will see these sanctuaries begin to come into existence and with new wisdom and beauty abound.

Maybe this new energy is more wisdom, understanding, and knowledge or when I tune into it, it feels beyond any of that. Perhaps all of our setbacks were for a good cause and truly we are entering into a time of higher consciousness. As I speak and read for many psychic friends, teachers and healers, we all seem to be heading towards a new inspiration, a new light, a new understanding, something new and different. Even though we may not be able to put it into words or understanding yet, it is close. Many times from very influential teachers and public icons have I heard it spoken, "I feel like I want to throw everything I have, everything I have learnt and teach and practice away, Shed it all and start anew!" Time and time again I have heard this and thought this myself. I believe it is now time to allow the new, to embrace the new light and understanding that is available now.

I believe it goes somehow like this. For decades, no, for centuries we have been learning, teaching, practicing, that Love will be the answer, the base of everything, the whole of everything. Everything. So we above all, jumped in and loved and sometimes, more often than not, we lost even ourselves at times and had to start over. We have loved being ridiculed, ripped off, abused and sometimes watched with love as our reputations, lives and souls were destroyed through others' overzealous power and ego displays and eventually, most of us, lost all of ourselves. We, lost everything, how many times have I heard this from people I believed should have known better. Love being the only worthwhile residue in all of it, in all of our experiences, because when you do love yourself, completely; it overflows onto and into everything else. You can't escape it. However, when we truly love ourselves we automatically learn discernment because when we love ourselves, we wouldn't submit ourselves to anything less. We do not feed our children, nor our inner child to the wolves. Yes, this is truth. Yes, with discernment we can see the truth.

Now we must learn to discern what is in fact, Truth!!! For if it is not truth don't waste your energy, when you know what is not real will fall away. We need to discern; if something or someone is true allow your energy of love to flow. If they or it is false, it always breaks down, and we lose our investment, quite often being ourselves.

Can you imagine just for a moment a world of empowered people, intelligent, discerning, loving and above all truthful!!! It really doesn't sound feasible. But watch as our governments, teachers, doctors, lawyers all become accountable. The truth is all that can save anyone or anything. Only the truth will prevail. No matter how much you love that lie, it will not sustain, because someone's truth will succeed. Yes, I hear you say, "And whose truth is more powerful than the other one is?" Yes, I know your truth and mine maybe different, but this is not my message. My message is, in the coming times it is about delving deeper than my fantasy or yours and cutting through all the dogma, perception fantasies and actually finding one truth, 'The Truth'. Then we can love or fear the truth, that is our choice, but above all when the Truth does prevail and it will, and it won't go away no matter how much you believe it will or how much you think you can change it. The Truth will sustain and sustain all those who welcome it and nurture and love it.

Look into your hearts and your souls' and open your minds and your eyes and see, feel, and know the Truth, it will set you free. It will bring you love and make you feel safe. In Truth you can have a wonderful life. A life in which you are free to express yourself and to enjoy in whatever way you feel you are at your best. A life in which you are free to be who you are.

Prayer and Meditation

G reat Divine Spirit and all that is, we ask in the name of God, for the presence of love, light and healing to be with us this moment. We ask that our Guides maintain our protection and we give thanks for all the special guides and angels and helpers which have come close, who will guide us along our path to enlightenment, truth and healing. May the light of God be with us, Amen?

Allowing your minds to relax now, and imagine a beautiful, peaceful and serene place, taking in some deep breaths. Breath in all that is good and kind and loving, and as you breathe out, let go. Let go of your daily routines, any problems and concerns, and all aches and pain, whether they be physical, emotional or mental. Just let them go, let go of everything and just be here and now.

As you breathe in, draw down the energy of Golden White Light. See it filling the room you are in. Know that it is the energy of the divine bringing protection, love and healing. Breathe in the essence of the divine, and as you breathe out, just let go. See and feel a beautiful pink light surrounding your physical body. Know that this light is the energy of self love, and will act as a magnet drawing out any negative energy, and anything you wish to let go of, now.

Relaxing and breathing in that divine white and gold light. Breathe the energy down through the crown chakra, through the third eye and down into the throat and the heart and lungs. Allow this energy to expand into your heart, relaxing your shoulders and neck and as you let go, breathe out any negative energy that you no longer need to hold onto. Whilst breathing in, expanding the light in your heart and lungs and allow the energy of light to flow down your arms and feel a tingling sensation in the tips of your fingers.

Take a deep breath and allow the energy to expand down into your abdomen, clearing and dissolving any negativity or pain and relaxing deeper and deeper. Allow the energy to flow down your legs and out through the souls of your feet, connecting you with Mother Nature.

When you breathe in, draw up the energy of Mother Nature, up through the souls of your feet, flowing through your legs and into your base chakra. Breathe the energy up through all the chakras and out through the crown chakra. Allow these energies to intermingle and cocoon you into a ball of light and energy, protecting you and keeping you safe.

Relaxing even deeper now.

Imagine in your mind's eye a place where there is calm and peaceful water. See yourself walking along and enjoying a star filled night and coming up on the horizon is a beautiful, large golden moon. Feel the energy that is being radiated out from this beautiful golden moon, see the peaceful sky and the twinkling stars and full moon rising above the horizon.

Now we are walking along a pier, a very long pier which is jutting out into the calm waters. See yourself walking out along this long pier, surrounded by water, you realize that you have left everything, your hand bag, your wallet and all your past, all your past experiences and conditioning behind. Let go and continue walking, out to the end of the pier, where you will meet up with a guide, a very special being or master who will give you directions and show you the next part of your journey. As you are standing or sitting with this wonderful being of light, watching the golden glistening of the moons' rays upon the water, a golden staircase will rise out of the water and go all the way up to this huge golden moon. This is your journey, enjoy and discover the magic and wonder of the universe. Be at peace and in Love.

About the Author

Reverend Judith Wilkinson—Zornig M.Msc. was born in Brisbane, Australia. Judith is a well known Psychic Clairvoyant, Medium and Channel and has been working in the spiritual arena since 1993. Judith was ordained in January 1995 as a Spiritualist Reverend, when she owned and managed a new age gift shop called The Enchanted Cottage. Judith has been studying her field for many years. Judith became a Reiki Master in 1996. Judith went on to study and train as a Swedish Massage Therapist and in more recent times, she has studied in depth Hypnosis and Past Life Regression with Dolores Canon, a well known American Hypnotherapist, Past Life Regressionist and Author. Also Judith is a Master Trainer of NLP (Neuro Linguistic Programming. She has been teaching meditation, Psychic Development, Tarot, Spiritual Healing and Philosophy, which is her main passion since the mid 1990's. Channelling is a natural gift as is her medium work. The book covers Insights on Life's Lessons and takes people on her life's journey trying to find the Truth as to why life is as it is, and hopefully helps people to solve the age old question that so many ask, *"Who Am I"* and *"Why am I here,"* and what life is really all about, in a simplistic easy to understand manner. Judith is an ordained Spiritualist Reverend, and has completed a Bachelor's and Master's Degree in Metaphysics with The University of Metaphysics and The University of Sedona, in the U.S.A. At present working on completing a Dissertation for PHD in Metaphysics.

In essence, Judith has spent her whole life searching for the answers, and sharing her findings with clients and congregations and friends. At last she feels she has a comfortable understanding of life and spirit, and hoping to introduce her spirit friends and guides through a new version of her book. Her newest spirit friend who she channels frequently likes to be known as the Lady of the Golden Rose, who lived a life as Mary

Magdalene. Judith likes to call her The Rose. The Rose has a light-hearted approach to presenting truths and insights and shows great compassion and understanding of the human experience. The Rose comes with a group of wonderful spiritual teachers and they are The Guardian of Eight. These beings give wonderful insights much the same as Abraham who is channelled by Esther Hicks. Esther Hicks is a very well known American Channel who channels Abraham, a group of beings from Source Energy. She is also the author of many books and DVD's.

You can contact Judith on email: judy.wilkinson@hotmail.com